MALACHI

GOD STILL LOVES YOU

The Proclaim Commentary Series

THE PROCLAIM COMMENTARY SERIES

MALACHI

GOD STILL LOVES YOU

VOLUME 39

MATTHEW STEVEN BLACK

PROCLAIM
PUBLISHERS

WENATCHEE, WASHINGTON

Malachi: God Still Loves You (The Proclaim Commentary Series)
Copyright © 2018 by Matthew Black
ISBN: 978-1-954858-08-4 (Print Book)
          978-1-954858-09-1 (eBook)

Proclaim Publishers
PO Box 2082, Wenatchee, WA 98807
proclaimpublishers.com

Cover art: *Prophet Malachi (Stained Glass)*
Church of St John's the Baptist, Hinton Charterhouse in Somerset, England

Ancient quotations (clearly marked with italics) have been at times changed to the ESV as well as some archaic language updated and additional phrases added for clarification. At times verse references (non-existent until recent times) have been interspersed as well to guide the modern reader.

First Printing, January 2018

Manufactured in the United States of America

Dedicated to Pastor Michael Tiberi, his wife Emily, and their precious daughter Eve who have poured out the love of God from their lives

CONTENTS

INTRODUCTION

God loved us not because we are lovable,
but because he is love.
C. S. LEWIS

There are times in the believer's life when he wonders: "Does God still love me?" The answer is: "Yes!" If we doubt God's love it is not because God has wandered, but that we have lost our way. A couple of songs of the church express the message of Malachi. The first is from the hymn, "Come Thou Fount of Every Blessing":

Prone to wander, Lord, I feel it,
Prone to leave the God I love;
Here's my heart, O take and seal it,
Seal it for Thy courts above.[1]

The second is from the modern worship song, "Wonderful, Merciful Savior":

Counselor, Comforter, Keeper
Spirit we long to embrace
You offer hope when our hearts have
Hopelessly lost the way.
Oh, we hopelessly lost the way! [2]

When God's people lose their way, he calls us back. He reminds us of his love and what true trust in his love looks like.

---

[1] Robert Robinson. "Come Thou Fount of Every Blessing." In John Julian. *A Dictionary of Hymnology* (London: John Murray, 1892), 252.
[2] Dawn Rogers. *Wonderful, Merciful Savior* (Nashville: Dayspring Music, LLC, 1989).

BACKGROUND

Malachi is the final book of the 12 Minor Prophets, which the Jewish scholars viewed as one book although recorded by 12 different scribes over a period of perhaps 350 years.[3] These 12 books are called minor not because they are less inspired or of less importance, but because the prophecies are shorter.

God loves his people, but because of their sins, his people (specifically the tribes of Judah and Benjamin) are taken into captivity by the Babylonians, with Jerusalem and the temple being destroyed in 586BC. A remnant of God's people returned from that captivity after 70 years and, during the time of the prophets Haggai and Zechariah, finished rebuilding the temple (520-516BC). After another 60 years Ezra arrived to further advance the nation. He was followed 13 years later by Nehemiah who rebuilt the walls of Jerusalem. There is therefore a general consensus of opinion that Malachi belongs to the same approximate period as Ezra and Nehemiah.[4]

Malachi's ministry takes place nearly a hundred years after the decree of Cyrus in 538BC, which eventually ends the Babylonian captivity and allows the Jews to return to their homeland and rebuild the temple (2 Chron 36:23). This was some 80 years after Haggai and Zechariah encouraged the rebuilding of the temple. Those two earlier prophets had said that the rebuilding of the temple would result in peace, prosperity, the conversion of people from other nations, and the return of God's own glorious presence (see Hag 2; Zech 1:16–17; 2:1–13; 8:1–9:17). To the discouraged people of Malachi's day, these predictions must have seemed a cruel mockery. In contrast to the glowing promises, they faced economic difficulties due to drought and crop failure (3:11). Things were difficult but not despairing. It was a time of stagnation – an uneventful waiting period. Judea remained an insignificant territory, no longer an independent nation and no longer ruled by a Davidic king. Worst of all, despite the promise of God's presence, they

---

[3] Portions of the background information adapted from André van Belkum. *Life, Hope, and Truth: Introduction to Malachi* and ESV online. *Introduction to Malachi.* Accessed 10 February 2017. https://www.esv.org/resources/esv-global-study-bible/introduction-to-malachi/

[4] Joyce G. Baldwin, *Haggai, Zechariah and Malachi: An Introduction and Commentary*, vol. 28, Tyndale Old Testament Commentaries (Downers Grove, IL: InterVarsity Press, 1972), 227.

experienced only spiritual decline. The days of Elijah and Elisha were passed. By Malachi's time, the Jews had been back in their homeland for more than a century. The temple had been rebuilt and the city of Jerusalem had been restored, but the promises of God were yet to be fulfilled. They felt like God had forgotten and no longer loved them.

AUTHOR

Not much is known about the author of this prophecy. We do know that he was a part of the Anshei Knesset Hagedolah, the Great Assembly that met in the Holy Temple in Jerusalem at the beginning of the Second Temple era.[5] "Malachi" simply means "messenger." This could be the name given to an anonymous book. There is a minority opinion in the Talmud that says that Malachi was actually Ezra the Scribe, a viewpoint adopted by Jerome and by Rabbi Rashi (1040–1105). Calvin was inclined to think that Malachi was Ezra's surname. There is no evidence that Malachi is to be identified with Ezra. There is another opinion that he was Mordechai from the story of the holiday of Purim. However, the opinion of the majority of the sages in the Talmud is that Malachi was a separate individual. The tradition is strong that Malachi is a personal name, and in the absence of compelling arguments to the contrary it is logical to accept that the prophet was called Malachi.[6]

DATE

Malachi was early on a contemporary of Esther (473BC). He would have seen the reforms of Ezra (458BC), and likely gave his prophecy during the absence of Nehemiah (433-424BC).[7] There are very few historical details in the Book of Malachi. The greatest clue as to its dating may lie in the fact that the Persian-era term for governor (*pehâ*) is used in 1:8.[8] This points to a post-exilic date of composition both because of the use of the Persian period term and because Judah had a king before the exile. Since, in the same verse, the temple has been rebuilt, the book

---

[5] Talmud, Bava Batra 15a and Megillah 17b.

[6] Theophane Chary. *Agge-Zacharie-Malachie* (Paris: Librairie Lecoffre, 1969), 223, 233, in Baldwin. *Malachi*, 227.

[7] H.L. Ellison, *From Babylon to Bethlehem. The People of God from the Exile to the Messiah.* (Exeter: The Paternoster Press, Ltd., 1976), 24.

[8] David W. Baker. *Joel, Obadiah, Malachi* (Grand Rapids, MI: Zondervan Publishing House, 2006), 208.

must also be later than 515BC. Malachi was likely written during Nehemiah's absence from Jerusalem when he returned to Persia for almost a decade (433-424BC).

Much of the background for Malachi is found in the books of his contemporizes (Esther, Ezra and Nehemiah). The context of Malachi is very much intertwined with Nehemiah. Malachi's emphasis in his prophecy demonstrates that he was carrying on the reforms that Nehemiah began. His emphasis on the law (4:4), coincides with a similar focus by Ezra and Nehemiah (cf Ezra 7:14, 25-26; Neh 8:18). They shared other concerns as well, such as marriages to foreign wives (2:11-15; cf Ezra chapters 9 and 10; Neh 13:23-27), withholding of tithes (3:8-10; cf Neh 13:10-14), and social injustice (3:5; cf Neh 5:1-13). Nehemiah came to Jerusalem (in 445BC), to rebuild the wall, and returned to Persia (in 433BC). He later returned to Israel (ca. 424BC) to deal with the sins Malachi described (Neh 13:6). So it is likely that Malachi was written during the period of Nehemiah's absence, almost a century after Haggai and Zechariah began to prophesy. Nehemiah returned for a second period as governor (ca. 424BC). Just a hundred years after Malachi's ministry (336BC), Alexander the Great would be proclaimed king of Greece and begin his conquest of the world. Malachi was most likely the last prophet of the Old Testament era (though some place Joel later).

After the completion of Malachi's prophecy, there were over 400 years of divine silence, with only Malachi's words ringing condemnation in their ears, before another prophet arrived with a message from God. That was John the Baptist preaching, "Repent, for the kingdom of heaven is at hand" (Mt 3:2). Messiah had come. Malachi is getting his generation and those that followed ready for that day.

THEOLOGY

The theology of Malachi for is vital and relevant for us today. This prophecy teaches us of the loving nature of God. We see the depravity of man in the cold expressions of dead religion. The people have a general knowledge of God but there is a great decline of godliness in all areas of life. Spiritual blindness is expressed with every accusation that questions the goodness of God. In a sense the theology of Malachi takes us back to Eden when the serpent caused Adam and Eve to doubt the loving nature of God. "Has God really said?" (Gen 3:1) is still the question on the lips of God's people in Malachi's day. God patiently explains his love to his disobedient people (1:2), and the rest of the book explain the realities of those who have genuine love for YHWH. The consistent message of Malachi and of the entire Bible is God's grace to sinners. He will save believing sinners (the righteous) and forsake unrepentant sinners (the wicked) when Messiah Jesus consummates the world in judgment (3:18; 4:1-3; *cf* Mt 25:31-33). Malachi's message is: God loves you, but do you love him? It is a wakeup call and invitation to be blessed and transformed by God's love.

Certainly, this prophecy is meant to encourage God's New Covenant people. "For whatever was written in former days was written for our instruction, that through endurance and through the encouragement of the Scriptures we might have hope" (Rom 15:4). The message of Malachi is as much needed today as it was in the dawning of the second temple. It is simply this: God is love. Because of his nature he will never forsake his people. He will continue to love us and through his word of rebuke and comfort, he will restore us back to Paradise, conformed to the original Imago Dei. That purpose can only be fulfilled through the promised messianic king so clearly proclaimed in Malachi's prophecy.

The need for Malachi's message and theology was direly needed in the beginning of the Second Temple period. The people had waited so long for God to fulfill his promises for Messiah, that the people had given up hope, become bitter, and even turned to idolatry and married pagan women. They had lost sight of God's loving nature. They saw him as aloof, uninterested and even unjust. The worship of God's people at that time was a cover for deep idolatry and serious fleshly addictions that cause the men to forsake their families and pursue pagan women and their lascivious worship.

Our day is no different. God's people need the refreshing words of Malachi to renew their love in a culture where iniquity abounds. Jesus said wherever lawlessness abounds, "the love of many will grow cold" (Mt 24:12). Only God through his Word can warm the hearts of his people. The book of Malachi does just that.

STYLE

Baldwin mentions that out of a total of fifty-five verses, forty-seven record in the first person the address of the Lord to Israel (the exceptions being 1:1; 2:11–15, 17; 3:16). This use of the first person presents a vivid encounter between God and the people, unsurpassed in the prophetic books.[9] Though sometimes Malachi is thought of as a book that lacks poetry and structure, its style is appropriate and effective for its message. The forthright style of the prophecy is not meant to be primarily inspiring or comforting, but convicting and alarming in order to wake the spiritually sleeping.

STORYLINE

The storyline of this prophecy is a conversation with God about his love for us and our love for him. It goes something like this:

Israel: God doesn't love us.

God: I have always loved you, but you haven't loved me.

Israel: How have you loved us?

God: You're still here aren't you? Edom and all the nations surrounding you are gone. I hated Esau, the father of the Edomites, but I have always loved you, and I still love you.

Israel: But do you really love us? We feel so deserted. We have waited so long for your promises, but nothing has happened. We're giving up and turning to other gods.

God: Indeed, I have always love you, but *you* have not love *me*. I have proven my love to you; it is time you prove your love for me. Here then is the outline for the prophecy of Malachi:

1. I have always loved you.
2. If you love me, enjoy my worship.
3. If you love me, lead my people.
4. If you love me, love your spouse.
5. If you love me, trust my timing.
6. If you love me, receive my blessing.
7. If you love me, serve my purpose.
8. If you love me, wait for my Son. I'm sending Jesus soon. You can be sure he is coming, because *I still love you.*

---

[9] Baldwin, 231.

And so the book of Malachi foreshadows the New Testament revelation where our Lord says, "If you love me, keep my commandments" (Jn 14:15). God loves us! And "we love him because he first loved us" (1 Jn 4:19, NKJV). In the following pages, we have an Old Testament theology of a living faith that expresses itself in love *for* God, fueled by love *from* God. Yet, more than a theology, the book of Malachi is a love letter to all Christians that stirs our hearts and minds to remember that when our love grows cold, God still loves us. He has always loved us, and it is the awakening of our souls to God's love that will renew our first love for him once again.

1 | Malachi 1:1-5

I STILL LOVE YOU

"I have loved you," says the Lord.
MALACHI 1:2

Many might wonder what a 2,400-year-old book can teach us. St. Paul reminds us: "whatever was written in former days was written for our instruction, that through endurance and through the encouragement of the Scriptures we might have hope" (Rom 15:4). Malachi is the last of what are called the 12 Minor Prophets of the Old Testament. They are minor only because of their length. The message of Malachi is simple and sweet. God says, "I have loved you" (1:2). The treatise is a compelling love letter to stir up our love in response to our infinitely loving God. Charles Haddon Spurgeon confessed his amazement at God's love: "Nothing binds me to my Lord like a strong belief in his changeless love. Thank God you have got a Father that can be angry, but that loves you as much when he is angry as when he smiles upon you."[10] God doesn't just give us a spare corner of his heart. The vast, entire, infinite, unfathomably loving heart of God belongs to you as God's born-again child. Malachi was called to deliver this message

---

[10] Charles Spurgeon. *Metropolitan Tabernacle Pulpit, Volume 35*, Sermon 2120, "The Security of Believers; or, Sheep Who Shall Never Perish" (London: Passmore & Alabaster, 1889), 685.

of God's love and favor to a people who were apathetic and blinded to his love.

The Role of Prophets in the Old Testament

Prophets have a very specific role in the Old Testament. First, prophets were preachers—*divine mailmen*. God would reveal his word to them, and they would publicly proclaim this word to the people un-edited. Typically, they were chosen to admonish and reprove God's people, denouncing their sin, threatening with the terrors of judgment, and calling people to repentance. This made them very unpopular.

Second, prophets were watchmen—*divine guards*. They guarded God's honor by warning against poor political decisions (2:11-12, like marrying pagan women), the dangers of idolatry and false worship (as a result of their pagan marriages), and the worthlessness of empty re-ligiosity and mere formalism (1:6-14). Malachi was God's divine guard-ian of godly society. Without Malachi's rebukes, the society of Israel would have disintegrated into moral, political, and social downfall, un-distinguishable from the pagan world around them.

Third, the prophets were attorneys for God – *divine lawyers* who would enforce and apply God's covenant to his people. Malachi makes a case against God's people for violating YHWH's law in various areas of life and society (2:1-9, on priests; 2:13-16, on marriage; 3:8-10, on tithing).

Fourth, prophets were also predictors—*divine future-tellers*. In addition to preaching and overseeing, prophets announced future judgments, deliverance, and foretold of the coming Messiah and his kingdom. From the prophecy of Malachi, we can we hear a call to repent of our empty worship (ch 1), a warning against our idolatry (chs 2-3), and a promise that God is sending the Messiah to save heal and save us from our sin (ch 4).

The Questions and Malachi

As a prophet, Malachi was a man chosen to represent God and speak for God. Malachi's prophecy consists of a series of questions God answers. These questions come from the minds of the people respond-ing to some of God's confrontations like: "I love you. Yet you have des-pised my name. You have polluted my covenant. You have wearied me with your complaints. You have robbed me. You have spoken against me." Israel responds. All of Israel's questions, or arguments, begin with *how*...

- *How* have you loved us?
- *How* have we despised your name?
- *How* have we tired you out with our complaining?
- *How* have we spoken out against you?
- *How* shall we ever return to you?

These people believe they have been faithful, and it is God who has let them down. They are truly blinded by their own spiritual pride. Instead of humbly accepting God's corrections, they judge God, not merely with their mouths, but in the depths of their hearts—just like us. How does a privileged people become so blinded to God's love? We could ask the same question today of ourselves. Why am I at times so blind to God's love? God's prophet Malachi answers that question for Judah and for us today. We don't know much about the prophet except that his name means, "God's messenger." He brings a message we desperately need to receive. In spite of my sin, God still loves me.

RECALL GOD'S LOVE FROM HIS WORD (1:1-2a)

In the book of Malachi, we have a people who did not feel loved by God. But they needed to know God loved them no matter the circumstances in their lives. You need to know God loves you no matter what your emotions are telling you. You are loved. This is how the prophet begins:

Malachi 1:1-2a | The oracle of the word of the Lord to Israel by Malachi.
     2 "I have loved you," says the Lord.

An unknown prophet named Malachi receives a word from the Lord called an oracle, literally translated "the burden" of the LORD. It is called a burden because there is weightiness to the message of this little book. It is a message intended to be heavy enough to transform the human heart. "Who shall separate us from the love of Christ? Shall tribulation, or distress, or persecution, or famine, or nakedness, or danger, or sword? ...No, in all these things we are more than conquerors through him who loved us. For I am sure that neither death nor life, nor angels nor rulers, nor things present nor things to come, nor powers, nor height nor depth, nor anything else in all creation, will be able to separate us from the love of God in Christ Jesus our Lord" (Rom 8:35, 37-39).

The message of Malachi is a call for true worship in response to his unrelenting love. "*I love you*" God says – "*you were created to love me. Worship me. Count my love as better than life.*" In order to transform sinners into worshippers, God reveals his heart. "I have loved you!" What a striking expression to hear God tell cold-hearted people: "I have loved you." God is not only describing his nature as a God who is love (1 Jn 4:8); he is declaring his eternal disposition toward his covenant people. "The Lord your God has chosen you to be a people for his treasured possession, out of all the peoples who are on the face of the earth. It was not because you were more in number than any other people that the Lord set his love on you and chose you, for you were the fewest of all peoples, but it is because the Lord loves you and is keeping the oath that he swore to your fathers.... Know therefore that the Lord your God is God, the faithful God who keeps covenant and steadfast love with those who love him" (Deut 7:6-9).

This love is not just for Israel of old, but for God's new Israel, with the peoples of every nation "grafted in" to Christ (Rom 11:17). I am part of God's "one new humanity" in Christ (Eph 2:15). I am seen by God through the merits of Christ. His love for me is not based on my favor, merits or power. He has chosen Israel (and me) precisely because I am weak and sinful so that he gets all the glory (*cf* 1 Cor 1:26ff).

God's people knew the words of Jeremiah from the beginning of their captivity, "Long ago the LORD said to Israel: 'I have loved you, my people, with an everlasting love. With unfailing love I have drawn you to myself'" (Jer 31:3, NLT), yet they still doubt. Astonishingly, the people responded: "In what way have you loved us?" (1:2). The love of God for his people is so great that it would seem to be beyond question, but these people doubted it. And many are questioning it today. We sometimes look beyond a thousand blessings to see one difficulty, and on the basis of our pain we doubt the love of God.

Refusing to let the doubt of Israel go unanswered, the Lord points to three phases of his love for them: God's love from the past (1:2b-3), his love in the present (1:3-4), and his love in the future (1:5). Why do they feel that God does not love them? A hundred years has passed since the second Jewish temple has been built and worship resumed. It has been 100 years since, through Zechariah, God promised to return to Jerusalem, to dwell in the city, to defend the city, and to institute peace and bring prosperity. God promised fruitfulness. God promised safety. God promised influence. God even promised respect from the world. The prophet Zechariah proclaimed, "Thus says the LORD of hosts: Peoples shall yet come, even the inhabitants of many cities. The inhabitants of one city shall go to another, saying, 'Let us go at once to entreat the favor of the LORD and to seek the LORD of hosts; I myself am going.' Many peoples and strong nations shall come to seek the LORD of hosts in Jerusalem and to entreat the favor of the LORD. Thus says the LORD of hosts: In those days ten men from the nations of every tongue shall take hold of the robe of a Jew, saying, 'Let us go with you, for we have heard that God is with you'" (Zech 8:20-23).

The people of Malachi's day have not experienced any of these things. The promises of God have not been realized in the time or way that they expected, therefore, in their eyes, God does not love them. Their families are suffering. They are surrounded by their enemies. They are barely paying their bills (so to speak), and they are mocked by the surrounding nations. Worship has been restored, but they are under the rule of a foreign king, so they begin to believe that God no longer loves them. In their mind, God walked away from his covenant of unrelenting love.

REMEMBER GOD'S LOVE FROM THE PAST (1:2b-3)

Thankfully, God does not leave them in their doubt. Our loving God answers their accusation that God no longer loves them. He tells them to understand his love, they need to realize they are still in their land. They still exist as a nation, unlike many other nations, including the Edomites, descended from Jacob's brother Esau.

Malachi 1:2b-3 | But you say, "How have you loved us?" "Is not Esau Jacob's brother?" declares the Lord. "Yet I have loved Jacob [3] but Esau I have hated. I have laid waste his hill country and left his heritage to jackals of the desert."

Jacob and Esau were not only brothers, they were twin brothers. Esau was born first, and customs dictated that Esau would be the heir of the father's blessings. But that is not what happened. Genesis 25 records how Jacob tricked Esau into selling him his birthright for a bowl of soup. Through deception, Jacob receives his father's blessing. And that is not the last time Jacob swindles someone. He proves himself to be quite the deceiver. Yet, God blessed him. God was not manipulated into blessing as a result of Jacob's deception. On the contrary, St. Paul gives a New Testament commentary:

> For this is what the promise said: "About this time next year I will re-turn, and Sarah shall have a son." [10] And not only so, but also when Rebekah had conceived children by one man, our forefather Isaac,[11] though they were not yet born and had done nothing either good or bad—in order that God's purpose of election might continue, not because of works but because of him who calls— [12] she was told, "The older will serve the younger."[13] As it is written, "Jacob I loved, but Esau I hated" (Rom 9:9-13).

God's love was fixed upon Jacob before he was born. In other words, God's love is *unconditional*. It is unearned and unmerited. This is consistent with how God revealed himself to Moses. Moses desired to see YHWH, and the Lord passed by and proclaimed his own name as "The Lord, the Lord, a God merciful and gracious, slow to anger, and abounding in steadfast love and faithfulness" (Exo 34:6). This is the announcement of the gospel in the Old Testament. God is primarily a God of mercy and grace and abounds in unrelenting covenant love and loyalty to the undeserving.

God's Love is Not Fair

God's love doesn't seem fair. Why does God love Jacob and hate Esau? We could ask, why am I saved but not my loved one or my friend? Grace is not fair. Unconditional love is not fair. If we want God to be fair, then he must cast us all into hell. But God set his love specially on Israel above all other nations. This was proof enough of his love. For them to be his people, they had to be chosen from among others, and the others had to be rejected.

The Lord reminds them of this by calling them to think about the patriarch Jacob and his brother Esau. How is it that Israel was in a spe-cial covenant relationship with God? It was because the Lord had made a choice. He chose Jacob and rejected Esau.[11] The Lord's statement that he "hated" Esau has caused no small amount of consternation among Bible students. What does it mean? A woman once said to Mr. Charles Haddon Spurgeon, pastor at the Metropolitan Tabernacle in London, "I cannot understand why God should say that he hated Esau." "That,"

---

[11] Roger Ellsworth. *Opening up Malachi* (Leominster, UK: Day One Publica-tions: 2007), 21.

Spurgeon replied, "is not my difficulty, madam. My trouble is to understand how God could love Jacob."[12]

Malachi 1:3 | Esau I have hated. I have laid waste his hill country and left his heritage to jackals of the desert.

God's love for Jacob (Israel) in the past had also been borne out by his providential care of her. While he had blessed her with the land of Canaan—'flowing with milk and honey'—the descendants of Esau (Edom) had been left without such a land.[13] In other words, the proof of God's love is that Israel still exists. They are not obliterated and cast into hell like other nations. Though they deserve to be judged, they are not condemned but under God's covenant of love.

The same is true of all new covenant believers in Christ, as seen by St. Paul's commentary of Malachi in Romans 9. We are loved by God's sovereign choice. He could just as easily have chosen Esau—Jacob's twin brother who holds the natural birthright. But God says, "I chose you, and passed Esau by." How has God loved Israel? God's answer is not what we expect. God says his love is not based on Jacob's performance, but on God's sovereign choice.

God loves us and saved us not based on anything in us. "But when the goodness and loving kindness of God our Savior appeared, he saved us, not because of works done by us in righteousness, but according to his own mercy, by the washing of regeneration and renewal of the Holy Spirit, whom he poured out on us richly through Jesus Christ our Savior, so that being justified by his grace we might become heirs according to the hope of eternal life" (Titus 3:4-7). Before the foundation of the world, before we could ever choose him, God chose us and ordained our lives to be "to the praise of his glorious grace" (Eph 1:4, 7).

God's Love is True Beyond Emotions

The modern Christian will often look to their own emotions and tend to question God's love in the same way as Malachi's hearers. We might ask: Why don't I feel loved? It is true for every believer that at times we do not "feel" loved by God. Emotions are complicated. We may love the Lord and at the same time doubt his promises. We are warned to "not lean unto your own understanding" (Pro 3:5), yet we

---

[12] William Newell. *Romans: Verse-by-Verse* (Grand Rapids: Kregel, 1994), 364.
[13] Ellsworth. *Malachi*, 21.

feel so distant from God. The New Testament calls us trust the Lord instead of being enslaved by the emotions and desires of our former life. We are called to walk not by our feelings but instead by faith in Christ. "When you heard about Christ and were taught in him... You were taught, with regard to your former way of life, to put off your old self, which is being corrupted by its deceitful desires; to be made new in the attitude of your minds; and to put on the new self, created to be like God in true righteousness and holiness (Eph 4:21-24). Our emotions are sometimes deceptive. If God's Word says he loves us, but our emotions say something different, we must not trust our emotions but instead trust the truth of God's word.

Though we are born again, we become confused about God's love for a number of reasons. Consider suffering and sin. In the context of Malachi, those in Jerusalem are hurting physically, emotionally, financially, materially, and in many other ways. Life is hard and somewhat hopeless—we will see that this doesn't result in anger but apathy in their relationship with God. When life is hard our thinking becomes foggy. Suffering, whether it is a major devastation or a minor disillusionment, has the power to lead us to doubt God's love. How do I know when I am doubting God's love? Generally, we begin by doubting the promises of God. We falsely believe that God is not *present* in our pain—he is not personally involved, does not care. We do not believe that God is in *control* of our pain – he is not strong enough to stop it. We do not believe he is *good* (especially if he is present and in control)—he is not loving enough to give us something better. We do not believe he has given us a *way of escape,* so we try to *control our pain* outside the will of God (sin).

A Warning About Your Feelings

Trusting our feelings leads to apathetic worship. Everyone has personal thresholds, some spoken and others unspoken, that lead to disbelief in God's love. Sometimes it is learning about thousands gassed in Syria, or thirteen people getting shot at a Navy base, or a faithful friend dying of cancer, or not having money to pay your bills, or losing your job, or a miscarriage, or a difficult marriage, or some other event that leaves us in state of hopelessness. Depression and even despair grip us, and we tend to trust our own distorted vision instead of putting on the spectacles of God's grace by reading his word. If we look through the lens of our own confused heart, we find it difficult to find and trust God, and almost impossible to worship God in our despair.

The Remedy for Your Despair

What is the remedy for our despair? How do I turn my focus onto God instead of my emotions? The root of despair is unbelief—a blindness towards the hope of God's promises. We will always be depressed and despairing if we look to ourselves. The answer is to look to the cross of Jesus. "Looking to Jesus, the founder and perfecter of our faith, who for the joy that was set before him endured the cross, despising the shame, and is seated at the right hand of the throne of God" (Heb 12:2). How has God demonstrated his love? "God demonstrates his own love for us in this: While we were still sinners, Christ died for us (Rom 5:8, NIV). He has done so by setting his heart on all believers before the world began. He chose them to be his own (Eph 1:4–6). We mere mortals cannot peer into the misty councils of eternity to see the electing love of God. So where do we look? To the cross of Jesus Christ! As we look there, we must each exclaim: God loved me so much that he nailed his Son to that cross to bear the penalty for my sins (Jn 3:16). "While we were still weak" and unable to save ourselves, "at the right time Christ died for the ungodly" (Rom 5:6).

God's Love is Displayed in the Cross

Sometimes our circumstances are such that we find ourselves wondering if God truly loves us, and the devil is ever eager to tell us that he does not. Our circumstances seem to prove it. But the wise believer points the devil to the cross and says, "There is where God proved his love for me, and my circumstances, whatever they mean, can never mean that God does not love me."[14] God's love is so strong, that he cannot help but sing of his love over you. "The LORD your God is in your midst, a mighty one who will save; he will rejoice over you with gladness; he will quiet you by his love; he will exult over you with loud singing" (Zeph 3:17). Until we can see the love of God in the suffering of Christ, we will continue to doubt God's presence, power and love when we suffer. To experience God's love, we must fix our eyes on Christ.

---

[14] Ibid, 22.

1. *In Christ we see that God is present in our sufferings.* God is not distant from our human experience—which is full of suffering. He entered into our suffering and lived for 33 years as a man, experiencing the hardship of life. And even though he was sinless, obeying and worshipping perfectly, he experienced temptation, sorrow, disrespect, poverty, rejection, mockery, abuse, and death. Jesus dwells with sinners. "For we do not have a high priest who is unable to sympathize with our weaknesses, but one who in every respect has been tempted as we are, yet without sin" (Heb 4:15).

2. *In Christ we see that God is in control of our suffering.* The hard life and the tragic death of Jesus did not surprise God; it was his plan. "This Jesus, delivered up according to the definite plan and foreknowledge of God, you crucified and killed by the hands of lawless men" (Acts 2:23). Though Jesus suffered at the hands of Romans, Jews, even family and friends, God was always in control. Jesus willingly suffered for sinners. God was in control of Jesus' suffering, and he's in control of yours. He has a good purpose for our suffering. "And the God of all grace, who called you to his eternal glory in Christ, after you have suffered a little while, will himself restore you and make you strong, firm and steadfast" (1 Pet 5:10, NIV).

3. *In the cross of Christ, we see that God is good in our suffering.* You will never believe that God loves you until you see the mercy that God has shown you through the love of Jesus Christ. When the child of God suffers, it is only for discipline, like a chisel crashing down on the marble of a great masterpiece. As C.S. Lewis said, "Pain insists upon being attended to. God whispers to us in our pleasures, speaks in our conscience, but shouts in our pain: it is his megaphone to rouse a deaf world."[15]

Pain is one way God gets our attention. The Christian's pain always has a good purpose. There is no condemnation for the child of God (Rom 8:1). God intends our pain as a blessing to meld us more into practical union with Christ. God doesn't give us what we deserve (hell), but he does give what we deserve to someone else—his own Son. To preserve his pure justice, sin must be punished. The child of God never suffers the punishment of his or her own sin. Never! Jesus paid it all. Now, in order to proclaim the Father's love, sinners must be forgiven.

---

[15] C. S. Lewis. *The Problem of Pain, Collected Letters of C.S. Lewis* (San Francisco: HarperCollins, 92.

God shows us mercy by sending his Son to die in our place. Until you can see that your present pain is nothing compared to the pain you actually deserve—you'll always question God's love. As Christians, we do sin (1 Jn 1:8), and sometimes God sends pain to discipline us (Heb 12:6), but never to punish us. God sends pain to save and sanctify us, for we are continually battling with sin, even as born again saints of God. Remember the words of our Lord: "Those who are well have no need of a physician, but those who are sick. I have not come to call the righteous but sinners to repentance" (Lk 5:31-32). He didn't come to condemn the lost, but to save them (Jn 3:17). He uses each trial, pain and even failure that we go through not to condemn us, but through the cross to work "all things together" for our good to conform us to Christ (Rom 8:28-29). We say thank you to God for the pain that comes to sanctify and preserve us for his heavenly kingdom.

REJOICE IN GOD'S LOVE IN THE PRESENT (1:3-4)

God not only displayed his love to Israel in the past, but now in the present he was showing them kindness, favor, and covenant faithfulness. Israel's neighbor to the south, Edom, was destroyed, never to rebuild again, but God protected Israel and brought her back to her homeland.

Malachi 1:3-4 | Yet I have loved Jacob but Esau I have hated. I have laid waste his hill country and left his heritage to jackals of the desert. If Edom says, 'We are shattered but we will rebuild the ruins,' the Lord of hosts says, 'They may build, but I will tear down, and they will be called 'the wicked country,' and 'the people with whom the Lord is angry forever'.

Both the descendants of Jacob (Israel) and Esau (Edom) had experienced tough times. Israel had spent seventy years in captivity in Babylon, and Edom had been invaded by the Nabateans[16] and forced from their land to take refuge south of Judah. But while God, in his love for Israel, was in the process of enabling Israel to rebuild her nation, he was doing no such thing for Edom. God's judgment was continuing to rest on Edom because of her refusal to see his grace at work in the life of Israel and to submit to it. That refusal revealed Edom to be a very

---

[16] A very powerful Arabian nomadic tribe that occupied the Sinai peninsula (the land peninsula between Egypt and Israel) all the way to the southern border of Israel from 4th century BC to 106 AD.

wicked nation and caused the Lord to have indignation against her. While God's love is most definitely a thing he demonstrated in the past, it is not only in the past. Every child of God drinks from the fountain of his love every day. St. Paul says we are blessed with every spiritual blessing in heavenly places in Christ (Eph 1:3). What are some of those blessings in the present that cannot be undone by the trials of the present?

- The truths of his Word
- The joys of fellowship with his people
- The beauties of his worship
- The assurance of his presence
- Daily expressions of his ongoing love
- His continuing willingness to forgive
- His guidance
- His readiness to hear our prayers
- His sustaining care

These things, richly enjoyed by the people of God, are not experienced by those who do not share their faith.

REST IN GOD'S LOVE FOR THE FUTURE (1:5)

God was faithful to Israel in the past and in the present, and YHWH will be faithful to her in the future in a marvelous way.

Malachi 1:5 | Your own eyes shall see this, and you shall say, "Great is the Lord beyond the border of Israel!"

This verse promises to Israel the coming of a better day. When would this better day come? Some think it refers to the time of the Maccabean dynasty when the Jews would successfully resist the power of the Grecian Empire and regain some of their former glory. But the ultimate fulfilment of this promise must be found in the Lord Jesus Christ. Through his redeeming work on the cross, and the sending of the Spirit of God on Pentecost to the Jews and then to all nations, he has caused us to say, "Great is the Lord beyond the border of Israel!"

The very fact that millions attend church each week to honor Christ constitutes proof that this promise has been and is being fulfilled. But the promise is going to reach its final fulfilment when the heavenly host and the redeemed of all ages and nations gather round the throne of God in praise for Christ's redemption. Gathered will be "a great multitude that no one could number, from every nation, from all tribes and peoples and languages, standing before the throne and before the Lamb" (Rev 7:9). That will be as far beyond the borders of Israel as one can get! That will also be a day when the people of God 'shall see' and 'shall say.' A day of seeing and saying! What will they see? There will be so much to see in eternal glory, but the most impressive of all is the seeing of the face of Christ (Rev. 22:4). And the seeing of our Redeemer will surely cause the redeemed to say:

> Worthy is the Lamb who was slain to receive power and riches and wisdom, and strength, and honor and glory and blessing! (Rev 5:12)

When I was a student at Ponchatoula High School in Louisiana, one of my most transformative and life shaping-classes was Art class with Mrs. Kim Zabbia. One of the lessons she taught me that if I wanted to replicate an object, I had to be totally committed to it. I had to get my eyes and my mind off myself and with my pencil, replicate each part of the object with its minute details. I had to be committed to every detail, every turn and shape of that object. I had to get my eyes and my mind off myself and on to that object, taking in every detail into my mind, and drawing it with my hand.

This is the secret to the experiencing the love of God. If you get your eyes off yourself and onto Christ, you will get your happiness from the Lord. Dear child of God, you are in Christ. God has a vision that is so much greater than yours. God is infinite, outside of time. He sees you as you will be in his presence, perfected and complete in Christ. You are complete right now in Christ (Col 2:10). He's applying His chisel in a thousand ways in your life – through trials and pain and difficulties – in weakness, in difficult relationships, in difficult circumstances. Throughout my life I have struggled with the idea of the love of God. I can preach and teach about it, but we all must accept it by faith. "We know how dearly God loves us, because he has given us the Holy Spirit to fill our hearts with his love" (Rom 5:5, NLT).

Conclusion

Like God's people in Malachi's day, you may not see the many evidences of God's love. God told his people then: you're still here – you have not been judged. So it is with you and me today. We deserve to be in hell. God has preserved us in order to save us. In all your sin and failure, God loves you. He calls you to embrace his love. Malachi says to God's people then, and to us today: God still loves you, but do you love him? Do you have faith in him? Do you trust him?

The rest of the book of Malachi is designed to examine your love for God. He's going to say, "If you love me, enjoy my worship, lead my people, love your spouse, trust my timing, receive my blessing, serve my purpose, wait for my Son. I still love you, but do you love me?" That's an important question to ponder.

2 | MALACHI 1:6-14

IF YOU LOVE ME, ENJOY MY WORSHIP

*A son honors his father, and a servant his master. If then I
am a father, where is my honor? And if I
am a master, where is my fear?*
MALACHI 1:6

This section of Scripture (1:6-14) is directed to the priests of Israel. In Malachi 1:1-5, God says "I have loved you Israel!" They question God's love, so Malachi "turns the tables" on their complaint. It is not God's love for Israel which is to be questioned, but Israel's love for God.[17] How vital it is to have leaders that love the Lord and "set the believers an example in speech, in conduct, in love, in faith, in purity" (1 Tim 4:12). An example is a prototype, a mold to be duplicated. Peter tells those who are pastors and elders to "shepherd the flock of God that is among you, exercising oversight, not under compulsion, but willingly, as God would have you; not for shameful gain, but eagerly; not domineering over those in your charge, but being examples to the flock. And when the chief Shepherd appears, you will receive the unfading crown of glory" (1 Pet 5:2-4). What if everyone in the church did exactly as you do? What would the church look like? Malachi is saying, the first

---

[17] G. P. Hugenberger, *Malachi.* In D. A. Carson, R. T. France, J. A. Motyer, & G. J. Wenham (eds.), *New Bible Commentary: 21st century edition* (Leicester, England; Downers Grove, IL: Inter-Varsity Press, 1994), 885-886.

way that we can show love to him is to show honor to God in your worship. When the love of God pierces the heart of a sinner, there is deep awe and reverence.

HONOR GOD WITH YOUR REVERENCE (1:6a)

The first way that we show love to God, according to Malachi, is to demonstrate honor to God in our worship.

Malachi 1:6, 14b | A son honors his father, and a servant his master. If then I am a father, where is my honor? And if I am a master, where is my fear? says the Lord of hosts to you, O priests, who despise my name. But you say, 'How have we despised your name?'...For I am a great King, says the Lord of hosts, and my name will be feared among the nations.

The leaders have drifted away from their fellowship with God, and it is seen in their lack of awe and reverence for God. True love for God is displayed in deep, reverent fear and humility that surpasses even the most revered human relationships (a son to his father, a servant to his master, a subject to his king).

Three relationships are mentioned that Malachi deems worthy of honor: father, master, and king. What a precious relationship – *father* and son. So tender. So filled with reverence for the tender Father. Unlike our earthly fathers, God our Father is perfect. He perfectly loves. Perfectly provides. Perfectly knows. Perfectly shepherds. He is due honor because he is good and worthy of honor. As the perfect Father, he loves us with "an everlasting love" and is due our worship and praise (Jer 31:3). A *master*, employer, owner of a company receives a measure of reverence and respect. He provides for and looks after the employees. As a perfect Master, our Lord perfectly provides for us and leads us into "paths of righteousness for his name's sake" (Psa 23:3). A great *king* or governor is to be reverenced and honored with allegiance. In earthly nations, we salute our flag and honor our president/governor/prime minister. As the King of kings, our Lord is owed our unconditional allegiance. Unlike the leaders of our world, he is perfect. He perfectly rules. He is perfectly wise, perfectly just, perfectly powerful, and perfectly protective. As our gracious and omnipotent King, he rules us for our good and his glory. He even shares his authority with us as "heirs of God and joint heirs with Christ" (Rom 8:17). The connecting link between the relationships of father, master, and king is one of reverence and obedience. God says, "Where is my reverence?" The people of Malachi's day had little to no reverence for God and were bored with his worship. They disregarded God's commands. They were careless in their worship because they did not love God.

Reverence: Recognizing of God's Greatness

Reverence is "the loving, sincere and practical recognition of the greatness of God."[18] It is to practice the presence of God. We might simply call it "the fear of the Lord." "The fear of the LORD is the beginning of wisdom, and the knowledge of the Holy One is insight" (Pro 9:10). Spurgeon said, "The fear of God is the death of every other fear; like a mighty lion, it chases all other fears before it."[19]

How do we practice God's presence so that we might reverence him as Malachi says we ought? We might think of a Latin phrase that summarizes what reverence means: *coram Deo*. According to R. C. Sproul, to live coram Deo "is to live one's entire life in the presence of God, under the authority of God, to the glory of God. To live in the presence of God is to understand that whatever we are doing and wherever we are doing it, we are acting under the gaze of God. God is omnipresent. There is no place so remote that we can escape His penetrating gaze."[20] Where ever you find the one who fears the Lord, you find an obedient heart. Obedience is the outflow of reverence. You reverence God by reflecting him. As believers in Christ, our goal is to "glorify God and to love him forever" (Question 1, Westminster Shorter Catechism).[21] To glorify means "to give the right opinion of" someone or something. The purest form of worship is to glorify God by reflecting him in holy obedient living.

One who fears God responds to God's Word with sober obedience. "But this is the one to whom I will look: he who is humble and contrite in spirit and trembles at my word" (Isa 66:2). Holiness and obedience flows from our worship and our awareness of his gaze. As regenerate people with new hearts God give us his Spirit to cause us to "walk in his statutes and keep his judgments" (Eze 36:25-27). Our Lord says, "If you

---

[18] Ellsworth, 27.

[19] Spurgeon. *Pulpit, Volume 13,* Sermon 748, "Self-Humbling" (1867), 241.

[20] R.C. Sproul. *In the Presence of God* (Nashville: Thomas Nelson, 1999), xiii.

[21] Westminster Shorter Catechism, https://www.opc.org/sc.html. Accessed 31 March 2017.

love me, keep my commandments" (Jn 14:15). "But why do you call me 'Lord, Lord,' and do not do the things which I say?" (Lk 6:46). Scripturally and theologically, right worship and obedience always go hand in hand. C. H. Spurgeon articulated how right living flows out of a regenerated heart: "Remember that if you are a child of God, you will never be happy in sin. You are spoiled for the world, the flesh, and the devil. When you were regenerated there was put into you a vital principle, which can never be content to dwell in the dead world. You will have to come back, if indeed you belong to the family."[22]

Reverence: Begins with Repentance

You may be discouraged because of the sin that seems to so easily beset you (Heb 12:1-2). Don't be discouraged. Let us not forget that God is unrelenting in his love, willing to forgive us and restore us when we sin. Reverence begins with repentance. Remember the promise first given to Solomon for Israel: "if my people who are called by my name humble themselves, and pray and seek my face and turn from their wicked ways, then I will hear from heaven and will forgive their sin and heal their land" (2 Chron 7:14). This promise can be applied to us today. God will forgive and heal us if we repent. St. John gives us the same promise in the New Testament: "If anyone does sin, we have an advocate with the Father, Jesus Christ the righteous. He is the propitiation for our sins, and not for ours only but also for the sins of the whole world" (1 Jn 2:1-2). He gives you the gift of perseverance if you are a child of God (1 Jn 5:2-5; Phil 1:6, 2:12-13). What is keeping your heart cold and your worship dead? Is it your sin? Receive God's promise to forgive you and experience his love anew right now.

HONOR GOD WITH YOUR BEST (1:6b-8)

"Do you love me?" God says. Give God your best. Put God first. Never give God the leftovers.

Malachi 1:6b-8 | But you say, 'How have we despised your name?' By offering polluted food upon my altar. But you say, 'How have we polluted you?' By saying that the Lord's table may be despised. When you offer blind animals in sacrifice, is that not evil? And when you offer those that are lame or sick, is that not evil? Present that

---

[22] Spurgeon. *Pulpit, Volume 32*, Sermon 1933, "Your Rowers Have Brought You Into Great Waters" (1886), 661.

to your governor; will he accept you or show you favor? says the
Lord of hosts.

Even though God declares "*I love you*," the people of Israel don't
believe him, and their attitude toward him in worship evidences that.
A cold heart has replaced reverence with bitterness, and instead of giving God our best when we are cold, we give him careless, coldhearted,
distant worship, that is really not worship at all, but a superficial formalism. God tells the Israelites they are despising his name by pollut-
ing the place of worship with worthless offerings. Specifically, the people are bringing God their leftovers. Instead of offering the best of their
flocks, they brought the blind, lame, and sick animals to the priests to
offer as sacrifices for their sin. God holds the priests responsible for
allowing the people to offer unacceptable sacrifices (1:7-8). The priests
were responsible to protect the purity of worship so as to *not* profane
God's name. Instead of praising God, they were complaining to God.
God's name is to be *worshipped*; instead the people were *whining*.
They were supposed to bring their best to God, but instead they were
bringing their worst. They gladly offered as sacrifices the very animals
that were likely to die soon. Thus they were not really sacrificing anything valuable at all. By their sacrifices they devalued God, reflecting
that in their heart, they did not believe God was worthy of their best.
To drive his point home, the Lord tells them to try the same thing with
their governor, "Present that to your governor; will he accept you or
show you favor? says the Lord of hosts" (1:8). No political leader of that
day would have been pleased with his people paying their taxes with
diseased animals. They would not even try to get by with such a thing!
But they were doing it with their supreme ruler![23] If all of life is worship, we must consider what our lives declare about God's value? Is he
valuable enough to deny myself anything this world might have to offer,
even my own comfort?

Remember what David said to Araunah when he wanted to sacrifice to God to stop his wrath against the people: "No, but I will buy it
from you for a price. I will not offer burnt offerings to the LORD my
God that cost me nothing." So David bought the threshing floor and the
oxen for fifty shekels of silver" (2 Sam 24:24). Indeed the love of Christ
is worth giving up all we have and all we are. "Whoever loves father or

---

[23] Ellsworth, 27.

mother more than me is not worthy of me, and whoever loves son or daughter more than me is not worthy of me. And whoever does not take his cross and follow me is not worthy of me. Whoever finds his life will lose it, and whoever loses his life for my sake will find it" (Mt 10:37-39). So we must ask ourselves:

- Is the Lord valuable enough for me to give up my money?
- Is the Lord valuable enough for me to give up my time?
- Is the Lord valuable enough for me to give up my food (i.e. 1 Cor 7 – *fasting*)?
- Is He valuable enough to give up my reputation?
- Is He valuable enough for me to give up my power?
- Is He valuable enough for me to give up my reputation?
- Is He valuable enough for me to give up my life?

St. Paul counted all privileges and blessings as loss for Christ. "But whatever gain I had, I counted as loss for the sake of Christ. Indeed, I count everything as loss because of the surpassing worth of knowing Christ Jesus my Lord. For his sake I have suffered the loss of all things and count them as rubbish, in order that I may gain Christ and be found in him, not having a righteousness of my own that comes from the law, but that which comes through faith in Christ, the righteousness from God that depends on faith—that I may know him and the power of his resurrection, and may share his sufferings, becoming like him in his death" (Phil 3:7-10).

We are to give our entire being as a love response to the Lord. This was the pinnacle of St. Paul's call to believers. How should we respond to the love of God given in Christ? "Therefore, I urge you, brothers and sisters, in view of God's mercy, to offer your bodies as a living sacrifice, holy and pleasing to God—this is your true and proper worship. Do not conform to the pattern of this world, but be transformed by the renewing of your mind. Then you will be able to test and approve what God's will is—his good, pleasing and perfect will" (Rom 12:1-2).

The response to Christ's love is so drastic, that the apostle equates it to attending his own funeral in order to live wholly for Christ. "I have been crucified with Christ and I no longer live, but Christ lives in me. The life I now live in the body, I live by faith in the Son of God, who loved me and gave himself for me" (Gal 2:20). C.T. Studd, missionary to Africa, India, and China concluded: "If Jesus Christ be God and died for me, then no sacrifice can be too great for me to make for him."

HONOR GOD WITH YOUR PRAYER LIFE (1:9)

God wants his people to honor him with a life of humble prayer, but only with a contrite heart. God rejects the prayers of the proud.

Malachi 1:9 | And now entreat the favor of God, that he may be gracious to us. With such a gift from your hand, will he show favor to any of you? says the Lord of hosts.

God does not want his people to "entreat his favor" if they have a cold heart. He doesn't want to hear hypocritical prayers. God's people then, like many today, had a cold, dead prayer life. Leonard Ravenhill said, "a man who kneels before God will stand before men." And again, "No man – I don't care how colossal his intellect – no man is greater than his prayer life."

What a privilege to talk to God personally. We are no longer his enemies, but he calls us friends! The wonder of salvation is that it is personal. J.I. Packer says in his book, Knowing God, that the main thing about prayer is not us opening up to God, but him opening up to us. Listen to Packer: "Knowing God is a matter of personal dealing... Knowing God is more than knowing about him; it is a matter of dealing with him as He opens up to you, and being dealt with by him... Friends open their hearts to each other by what they say and do. We must not lose sight of the fact that knowing God is an emotional relationship, as well as an intellectual and volitional one, and could not indeed be a deep relationship between persons if it were not so."[24] "What is prayer, then, in the fullest sense? Prayer is continuing a conversation that God has started through his Word and his grace, which eventually becomes a full encounter with him."[25]

The people of Malachi's day had a disdain for the name of God that resulted in God refusing to answer their prayers. Malachi seems to dare the priests to check this out for themselves. He essentially says, "Ask God for something. See if he will be gracious." He then solemnly assures them that they cannot ask for God's favor with their mouths while their hands are engaged in dishonoring him. We do not like to be told

---

[24] J. I. Packer, *Knowing God* (Downers Grove, IL: InterVarsity, 1993), 39– 40.
[25] Tim Keller. *Prayer* (London: Penguin Books, 2014), 48.

that the success of our prayers is tied to the conduct of our lives, but it is a link that the Bible will not let us ignore (Prov 15:29; 28:9). "If I had cherished iniquity in my heart, the Lord would not have listened" (Psa 66:18). "Behold, the Lord's hand is not shortened, that it cannot save, or his ear dull, that it cannot hear; but your iniquities have made a separation between you and your God, and your sins have hidden his face from you so that he does not hear. For your hands are defiled with blood and your fingers with iniquity; your lips have spoken lies; your tongue mutters wickedness" (Isa 59:1-3).

Our first response to unanswered prayer, therefore, must not be to accuse God of failing to keep his Word but rather to examine our hearts to see if we are living according to his Word.[26] This doesn't mean we have to be perfect in order to get our prayers answered. We must clear the channel between God and ourselves if we expect his blessings to flow to us. One commentator, John Benton, observes: "God's answering our prayers does not depend on our being sinless. If this were the case no one would have their prayers answered, for none of us is perfect this side of heaven. However, God's hearing our prayers does depend on our being serious about the fight against sin in our lives. It is not the presence of sin but the *toleration* of sin which shuts down communication with heaven."[27]

HONOR GOD WITH YOUR HEART (1:10)

God's message through Malachi is that worship matters. It has been a hundred years since the scattered Israelites returned home to gather; a hundred years since they rebuilt the temple; a hundred years since they appointed priests and began to worship and make sacrifices. Nehemiah 12 records the day when the people rededicated the walls of the city and restored the first services in the temple. The priests were assembled, instruments were gathered, and two great choirs sang as they walked along the walls of the city.

"And they [*the men of Israel*] offered great sacrifices that day and rejoiced, for God had made them rejoice with great joy; the women and children also rejoiced. And the joy of Jerusalem was heard far way" (Neh 12:43). In all the excitement, people were eager to serve. Some

---

[26] Ellsworth, 32-33.

[27] John Benton. *Losing Touch with the Living God: Malachi*, Welwyn commentary series (Wyoming, MI: Evangelical Press, 1993), 53.

signed up to manage the storerooms, others to sing on the worship team, a few to administrate the finances, and even a couple to act as security at the gate. "And all Israel in the days of Zerubbabel and in the days of Nehemiah gave the daily portions for the singers and the gate-keepers; and they set apart that which was for the Levites; and the Levites set apart that which was for the sons of Aaron" (Neh 12:47). Worship was an important time of great joy, great unity, and great sacrifice for both the priests and the people.

Malachi takes place a hundred years after Nehemiah, and things are different now. Attitudes have changed. Israel is no longer zealous for worship. In only a hundred years, two generations, worship has become heartless and obedience unimportant. Neither the priests nor the people are excited about worship. It has become a routine, a checked box, a joyless duty. Having not experienced the prosperity they expected, the Israelites find themselves disillusioned about their lives and doubtful about God's promises. Even though God declares "*I love you*," they don't believe him, and their attitude toward worship evidences that. Anytime men declare, by word or deed, that worship "isn't worth it," they in fact declare that God is not worthy to be honored or obeyed.

God shocks them by asking them to shut the church, basically. *Stop worshipping me at my temple. Don't come anymore.* God says:

Malachi 1:10 | Oh that there were one among you who would shut the doors, that you might not kindle fire on my altar in vain! I have no pleasure in you, says the Lord of hosts, and I will not accept an offering from your hand.

This verse adds yet another catastrophic result of the priests' irreverence. Here the Lord tells them that their worship is *worthless* in his eyes. God calls them to shut the doors of the temple. God says, "No worship is better than unengaged worship!" We cannot read the Lord's words here without thinking of the similar message delivered by the Lord Jesus to the church of Laodicea: "I know your works, that you are neither cold nor hot. I could wish you were cold or hot. So then, because you are lukewarm, and neither cold nor hot, I will spew you out of my mouth" (Rev 3:15–16). Lukewarm worship causes God to vomit.

This must not be used as an excuse not to worship. God commands both that we worship him and that we worship him in the right way. And the right way is, of course, that which the Lord Jesus indicated in his conversation with the Samaritan woman: "God is Spirit, and those who worship him must worship in spirit and truth" (Jn 4:24). "To worship God in spirit is to worship him with our *spirits engaged*. It is to worship with our hearts going out after God... To worship God in truth is to do so *according to what God himself has revealed*. It is to worship according to the truth of his Word." Worship from the heart and according to the Bible is the kind of worship that pleases God. We are not left to define worship for ourselves. The Lord Jesus has defined it for us.

HONOR GOD WITH YOUR TESTIMONY (1:11-12)

I ask my children almost every day, "What is the chief end of man." I love to hear our four-year-old Ava tell me! "To glorify God and to love him forever." This is the first question in the Westminster Shorter Catechism. St. Paul says, "Whether you eat or drink or whatever you do, do all to the glory of God." To do all to his glory literally means, "to give the right opinion" of God. God's people were not giving the right reflection and opinion of God. Yet God says he will get glory. The people of Israel could not imagine a day like ours today where God gets glory wherever the sun shines! Listen to Malachi's prophecy:

Malachi 1:11-12 | For from the rising of the sun to its setting my name will be great among the nations, and in every place incense will be offered to my name, and a pure offering. For my name will be great among the nations, says the Lord of hosts. But you profane it when you say that the Lord's table is polluted, and its fruit, that is, its food may be despised.

A Testimony for All Nations

Twice in this verse the Lord says:

Malachi 1:11 | My name shall be great among the nations.

The Lord is absolutely committed to bringing glory to his name not just in your neighborhood or your borders but far beyond. God has a heart for the nations. Billions live in darkness without the knowledge of Christ. God's people care about evangelism and missions because

God cares about the nations. As John Piper likes to say, "Missions exists because worship doesn't" among the nations.[28] Our worship catapults missions. God's love burns in our hearts and sets us ablaze to reach the nations. Sadly, this was lacking in Malachi's day. The religious leaders of Malachi's day were refusing to give God glory, but they were not derailing God's plan. They were only hurting themselves. God did not need Israel to give him glory. God's ultimate plan was never for the tiny nation of Israel alone. God is "not wishing that any should perish, but that all should reach repentance" (2 Pet 3:9).

If Israel would not give him his due, he would receive it from the Gentiles – on such a wide scale that it was possible for him to say that he would be receiving glory all the time ("from the rising of the sun, even to its going down") and in "every place" (1:11). The fullness of God's beauty and glory is revealed in the gospel. God is good. He sent his Son to open the door of salvation to all nations. Nothing brings God more glory than the good news of the gospel preached in all the world. The gospel is the good news of what God has done in and through his Son, Jesus Christ, to provide forgiveness of sins and eternal life for all who believe in Jesus. The heart of the gospel is Jesus' death on the cross. There he received the wrath of God in the place of sinners. Because he received it, those sinners never have to receive it. They are freed from the penalty of sin because Jesus endured it on their behalf.[29]

A Testimony that Transforms Others

This grand scale testimony is something that the priests of Israel were forfeiting. We need to pray for God's blessing to make our testimony go beyond our own comfort zone. Paul said the evidence that we have been touched by God's glory is a changed life that influences others. We now have the power to live an example and to imitate the Lord. 2 Corinthians 3:18 says as we gaze at Christ, we are changed into his image from one level of glory to the next.

Paul said a similar thing in 1 Thessalonians 1:6-10, "You became imitators of us and of the Lord, for you received the word in much affliction, with the joy of the Holy Spirit, so that you became an example to all the believers in Macedonia and in Achaia. For not only has the

---

[28] John Piper. *Let the Nations be Glad*, 3rd Edition (Grand Rapids: Baker Academic, 2010), 15.

[29] Ellsworth, 35.

word of the Lord sounded forth from you in Macedonia and Achaia, but your faith in God has gone forth everywhere, so that we need not say anything. For they themselves report concerning us the kind of reception we had among you, and how you turned to God from idols to serve the living and true God, and to wait for his Son from heaven, whom he raised from the dead, Jesus who delivers us from the wrath to come." Is this your testimony? Do you live like this? Is the central motivation of your soul to live a life to God's glory? Oh, that we would come to him with this kind of heart for his glory to be displayed among the nations!

A Testimony of Pure Offerings

Instead of a "pure offering," the priests of Judah offered a "profane" and "polluted" one.

Malachi 1:12 | But you profane it when you say that the Lord's table is polluted, and its fruit, that is, its food may be despised.

The worshippers in Israel had restored the temple worship but had allowed their hearts to become cold and their worship to become sloppy and careless. Instead of giving the correct offering from a pure heart, they were careless in the selection of animals and were giving God their leftovers. They "despised" having to perform these ceremonies and resented God for having to constantly offer sacrifices. There were five offerings in Leviticus that pointed to the sacrifice of Jesus Christ. All are described in Leviticus 1-7.

What kind of pure offerings are prescribed?

The offerings were considered pure if they were offered in accordance with the Levitical law and if the worshippers had a humble attitude.

The *burnt offering* was consumed entirely by the fire. The burnt offering teaches that God is pleased to accept anyone who comes to Him through His prescribed sacrifice (Lev 1:3). The whole animal was consumed on the altar, and it atoned for the worshipper's sin. It satisfied God's wrath against sin and made fellowship possible between a holy God and a sinful person.

The *grain offering* was given for the showbread. Someone accepted by God by his grace—through the burnt offering—could respond in gratitude through a grain offering (Lev 2:2). It usually was an offering of flour and oil in which a handful was burned and the priests ate the rest. It was a gift to God from the best of the worshipper's agricultural produce in an act of thanksgiving for sins forgiven. An additional offering, the drink offering (or "libation"), was poured on top of the grain offering as a symbol of joy (Lev 23:13; *cf* Exo 29:40-41). This reminds us that Jesus reconciles us to God and makes us his friends, for no one ever breaks bread with his enemies. We now break bread with Jesus as members of God's forever family.

The *peace offering* was a large offering, normally a bull or cow. It was to be eaten within two days, and not more than three, so it had to be shared with the community. Unlike the other offerings, the peace offering was optional, given in addition to the burnt offering. It was a festive offering reminding the worshippers that they have peace with God and with each other. There were three primary peace offerings: the thanksgiving offering—a freewill offering given as an act of thanksgiving to God when he blessed someone without their asking for it. Only in this instance could an imperfect animal be offered (Lev 7:12-15). The wave offering—the priest's portion of the peace offering was waved before the Lord as a special act signifying that it was his (Lev 7:30-31). The freewill offering—this was given because of a vow taken, or in relation to a favor, or a simple voluntary act of worship (Lev 7:16-17). So Jesus brings his people into community with each other as they partake of him.

Then there is the *sin offering*. Normally the sin offering was offered and burnt outside the camp (Lev 4:2-3). It was not to be eaten, but taken and burned outside the camp. This reminds us that Jesus became a curse for us and was cast out of Jerusalem and crucified outside the city at Golgotha, the place of the skull. Once a year on the day of atonement, the sin offering is a scapegoat, when all the sins of the people are transferred to the goat, and the goat wanders through the wilderness. So Jesus was forsaken of the Father and became our scapegoat.

Finally, there is the *guilt offering*. The guilt offering caused the individual to look beyond the sin to the damage it caused (Lev 5:16). The guilt offering is also called "reparation" because the person not only sought forgiveness, but first he or she also paid full restitution, adding to the price an additional percentage. This reminds us that we need to be constantly repenting in the Christian life. We do not need to offer bulls and goats continually since our Lord has been sacrificed "once for all" (Heb 10:10).

Because the offerings in Leviticus had their ultimate fulfillment in Jesus Christ, there is no need for them today (Hebrews 10:1-18). In fact, after Jesus sacrificed His life on the cross and rose again, the temple was destroyed in AD 70. No sacrifices have been made there since.[30]

What made their offerings polluted?

Instead of offering pure offerings as prescribed by the book of Leviticus with clean hands and a pure and loving heart, the people were annoyed by the constant need to sacrifice. While we as modern people can understand their distaste of continually offering bloody sacrifices, yet they lost their gratitude for God's forgiveness and polluted the offering by not only having a careless and hard-hearted attitude, they also brought sacrifices that were lame and deformed. They gave God the leftovers.

HONOR GOD WITH YOUR WORSHIP (1:13)

God asks: do you love me? Worship me with passion. Sometimes our flesh grows weary of worship. Our hearts become disengaged. We feel defeated before we ever enter the congregation of God's people. How can we reignite our worship? The people in the book of Malachi had the same need. They had grown so weary and cold-hearted. Only God's love can melt such stone-cold hearts.

Wounded Worship

Malachi 1:12 | But you profane it [my worship] when you say that the Lord's table is polluted, and its fruit, that is, its food may be despised. But you say, 'What a weariness this is,' and you snort at it, says the Lord of hosts.

The word "profane" comes from a Hebrew word which means "to wound or stab." What a word to use in connection with the glorious, precious name of God. Wounding it! Stabbing it! Through our pride, we wound the worship of God. We mangle it. Pride mangles everything.

Listen to the words of St. Aurelius Augustine, Bishop of Hippo (North Africa): "I was astonished that although I now loved You... I did

---

[30] Wayne Stiles. "Offerings in Leviticus: What They Were and Why They Mattered" (Aubrey, TX: waynestiles.com, 2012). Blog article: https://www.waynestiles.com/images/misc_downloads/Offerings%20in%20Leviticus%20Chart.pdf Accessed 30 Oct 2017.

not persist in enjoyment of my God. Your beauty drew me to You, but soon I was dragged away from You by my own weight and in dismay, I plunged again into the things of this world... as though I had sensed the fragrance of the fare but was not yet able to eat it."[31] When we lose our passion for worship, we backslide and are once again in bondage to the world and its desires. We become blinded to the beauty of Christ and exalt the world above Christ in our hearts. This is a serious danger for the child of God. Malachi calls this "wearisome worship" a "profaning of God's name."

Blind Worship

How were the priests profaning God's name? With their prideful attitudes and action. They were essentially declaring that the "table" (i.e. temple worship) of the Lord was contemptible, that is, something which possessed no appeal or value. The people of Israel were blinded to the fullness of worshipping the living God.

Malachi 1:13 | You bring what has been taken by violence or is lame or sick, and this you bring as your offering! Shall I accept that from your hand? says the Lord.

By bringing stolen, lame and sick animals, they were effectively proclaiming that they put no value at all upon their worship of the Lord, that they regarded it as having no significant meaning for their lives.[32] It was mere formalism, "having the appearance of godliness, but denying its power" (2 Tim 3:5). J.C. Ryle spoke to this over a hundred years ago: "Look for example at those thousands of people whose whole religion seems to consist in keeping religious ceremonies and ordinances. They attend regularly on public worship. They go regularly to the Lord's table. But they never get any further. They know nothing of experimental Christianity. They are not familiar with the Scriptures and take no delight in reading them. They do not separate themselves from the ways of the world. They draw no distinction between godliness and ungodliness in their friendships or matrimonial alliances. They care little or nothing about the distinctive doctrines of the gospel. They appear utterly indifferent as to what they hear preached."[33]

---

[31] Aurelius Augustine. *Confessions* (London: Penguin Books, 1961), Book VII, paragraph 17.

[32] Ellsworth, 38.

[33] J.C. Ryle. "Formality," booklet (Pensacola, FL: Chapel Library, nd).

Wearisome Worship

The priests were also sinning against the name of the Lord by openly expressing their unhappiness about having to serve. As they went about their duties they were saying, "Oh, what a weariness!" To them the service of God was an irksome duty instead of a joyous delight.[34] As we go about public worship, do we give the impression that the things of God are exceedingly precious and glorious? Or do we give the impression that we are engaged in an unpleasant obligation that must be taken out of the way as quickly as possible? Do we go about our service to the Lord in such a way that we make it appear to be a very unattractive thing and in such a way that we make the things of the world to be very wonderful? Do we show respect for the preaching of God's Word? Or do we, by laughing and talking with those around us, show contempt for it?[35]

Satisfying Worship

By way of contrast, we read David's words in Psalm 63:1, and we see that he has lost himself in God. He says, "O God, you are my God; earnestly I seek you; my soul thirsts for you; my flesh faints for you, as in a dry and weary land where there is no water." You can see that David is done looking for anything in himself or in the world that will help or satisfy him. I think if we were transparent, we all would confess that we all want this deep soul satisfaction that David seeks. If you want it, you must forsake all and follow Christ as your God and your all. He must own you and you must claim him. It will cost you everything. Jesus said, "If anyone would come after me, let him deny himself and take up his cross and follow me" (Mk 8:34). We must go to our own funerals. A genuine Christian life is one of giving total and absolute allegiance to God and dying to self. You will never know God unless you die to self. As Amy Carmichael wrote:

> O Prince of Glory, who dost bring
> Thy sons to glory through the Cross,
> Let us not shrink from suffering,
> Reproach or loss.[36]

---

[34] Ellsworth, 39.

[35] Ibid.

[36] Amy Carmichael. Quoted by Joni Eareckson Tada. *Pearls of Great Price* (Grand Rapids: Zondervan, 2006), 178.

God will not be found without an end of self. Christianity from beginning to end is a call to die to self and to live to God. Before Jim Elliot left for Ecuador, from which he would never return because of martyrdom, he wrote his mother: "Remember we have bargained with him who bore a cross. Our silken selves must know denial."[37] We are so attracted to this life. We try to find satisfaction in it, but we will always come up empty. We must let go of this life once and for all. We must go to the cross and to the tomb to die. Yet the alternative is worth it all.

WHEN YOU HONOR GOD, HE BLESSES YOU (1:14)
Do you love me? Seek my blessing!

Malachi 1:14 | Cursed be the cheat who has a male in his flock, and vows it, and yet sacrifices to the Lord what is blemished. For I am a great King, says the Lord of hosts, and my name will be feared among the nations.

The opposite of this pronouncement is the blessing the Lord gives to the priests at the establishment of the Tabernacle. "The Lord bless you and keep you; the Lord make his face to shine upon you and be gracious to you; the Lord lift up his countenance upon you and give you peace" (Num 6:24-26).

Superficial worship never brings the blessing of God we all long for. In fact, superficial worship is dangerous because it brings a curse (the sign of God's rejection). To be cursed was no empty threat, therefore, but led to death, whereas the blessing bestowed life (Deut 30:19). The man who trifled with God in the Old Covenant would not go unpunished, but would find out that YHWH was in fact *a great King* as well as father and master (1:6) and that he did not spare those who flouted his majesty.[38]

When we honor God, we are truly blessed. As a great King, we are his sons and daughters, "heirs of God and fellow heirs with Christ" (Rom 8:17). The "blessed man... is like a tree planted by streams of water that yields its fruit in its season, and its leaf does not wither. In all that he does, he prospers. The wicked are not so, but are like chaff that the wind drives away" (Psa 1:3-4). Do you want God's blessing, worship him with all your heart. Hold nothing back. Stand alone if you must. Be

---

[37] Tada, *Pearls*, 5.
[38] Baldwin. *Malachi*, 251.

radical. We live only one very short life. "Love the Lord your God with all your heart and with all your soul and with all your strength and with all your mind" (Lk 10:27).

Conclusion

Remember, the theme of Malachi is God's unrelenting love. If we seek him and worship him as a great and merciful King, he will bestow his infinite and unrelenting love upon us, but if we do not honor him, we will one day meet him at his fearful tribunal as a King who brings only judgment. Oh, how he loves you. It is only right that if we love him, we enjoy his worship.

3 | MALACHI 2:1-9

IF YOU LOVE ME, LEAD MY PEOPLE

For the lips of a priest should guard knowledge, and people should seek instruction from his mouth, for he is the messenger of the Lord of hosts.
MALACHI 2:7

God says, "I have loved you!" But the people respond with the accusatory question: "but how have you loved us?" God's answer is "I have loved you, but you haven't loved me." And God zeros in on the leadership of the priests. "And now, O priests, this command is for you." He tells them "Listen to me and... honor my name" (2:1). God basically says, "You want to see love return to the people of God – it's up to the leaders to repent." Everything stands and falls on leadership. Scottish preacher Alistair Begg said it this way, "The church of Jesus Christ does not progress beyond the spiritual progress of its leaders."

God's command to the priests is simply: obedience. As New Covenant believers, we might say, your knowledge means nothing unless you "walk in the Spirit." Let God rule you. Be a living sacrifice. Surrender all. Hold nothing back. The priests were holding on to the false comfort of their lives. I like how Corrie Ten Boom put it: "Don't bother to give God instructions, just report for duty." Here the priests of Israel were questioning God instead of obeying him. A. W. Tozer said it well: "Have you noticed how much praying for revival has been going on of late - and how little revival has resulted? I believe the problem is that we have been trying to substitute praying for obeying, and it simply will not work." If we love God as leaders, we will love God with our lives. "Glorify me by listening and obeying me," God says. Everything stands and falls on leadership. This is why the Lord begins by addressing the priests.

HOW THE PRIESTS OF MALACHI RELATE TO US

Christ is the perfect and eternal Priest. He's our perfect High Priest. According to John Piper, "Christ is now the one and only priest between us and God. The reason for this is that his sacrifice was final and his life is indestructible (cf. Heb 7:16)."[39] "But when Christ appeared as a high priest ... he entered once for all into the holy places, not by means of the blood of goats and calves but by means of his own blood, thus securing an eternal redemption" (Heb 9:11-12).

Indeed, "Peter calls the whole church a "holy priesthood" (1 Pet 2:5) and a "royal priesthood" (1 Pet 2:9); and John says that Christ made the whole church a kingdom, priests to his God and Father (Rev 1:6). This means that Christ has opened the way for all of us to come directly to God through him. We do not need any human mediator. We can walk with Christ—our high priest—right into the Holiest Place where God dwells and find grace to help in time of need (Heb 4:16)."[40]

Duties of Priests in the New Testament

There is no official priesthood in the New Testament church. No church leaders are called priests because of their office in the church. But this raises the question: Were there other duties that priests had in the Old Testament besides offering sacrifices for the sake of the people—duties that may indeed be continued in the New Testament? The answer is a clear yes.

Malachi 2:7 | For the lips of a priest should guard knowledge, and people should seek instruction from his mouth, for he is the messenger of the Lord of hosts.

In other words the priests were teachers. This part of their ministry is continued in the church of the New Testament. Paul says that

---

[39] John Piper. Sermon, "The Curse of Priestly Failure" from Malachi 2. November 8, 1987, Bethlehem Baptist Church, Minneapolis, MN.
[40] Ibid.

Christ gave to the church some pastors and teachers to equip the saints for the work of the ministry (Eph 4:11-12). First Timothy says that there are to be overseers who are able in teaching (3:2) and that some elders in the church are to labor in preaching and teaching (5:17; cf. Titus 1:9).

So this part of the priests' duties in Israel is continued in the elders of the New Testament church today—they are responsible to teach and guide the church. But they are never called "priests." Yet Piper concludes that these duties of the priests (teaching and instructing of God's Word) are applicable to all of us and specifically to the elders of Christ's church. So this message is for anyone who is called to instruct God's people in the New Testament church. It is specifically addressed to anyone who would be a leader in God's church. We need to see the scope of the entire passage (2:1-9). The outline of this passage is a chiastic arrangement.

- 1-3, rebuke / judgement
- 4-7, prototype of true minister
- 8-9, rebuke / judgement

Who are the Priests?

The passage begins with a command addressed to the priests.

Malachi 2:1 | And now, O priests, this command is for you" (2:1).

Who exactly are the priests? The priests are from the tribe of Levi and directly descended from Aaron. While any Levite could help serve in the Temple, the priests were those who carried out two important duties: (1) The priests received and prepared the sacrifices from the people in the Temple. (2) The priests instructed the people on the Sabbath Day and other occasions.

God is severely offended at the priests. He curses them and removes his blessing upon them. God, the Great King, is not honored by their half-hearted actions and will not accept their offerings. He actually curses those who claim to worship fully but act as hypocrites and give sick animals. The priests are accepting these worthless offerings rather than instructing or correcting the people for their faithlessness. They complain and "snort" back to God that their role as the teacher-priest is making them weary because they are to live off the offerings and tithes of these faithless people. Now God shifts the conversation form the people to the leaders who are responsible for not upholding the purity of worship. It is here we can see the signs and evidences of leaders who are failing to lead God's people in a godly way.

THE PITFALLS FOR LEADERS (2:1-3, 8-9)

Everything stands and falls with leadership. The entire book of Malachi is filled with rebukes to the priests. Malachi indicted the false priests and the people on at least six counts of willful sin:

- Repudiating God's love (1:2-5);
- Refusing God his due honor (1:6 - 2:9);
- Rejecting God's faithfulness (2:10 - 16);
- Redefining God's righteousness (2:17 - 3:6);
- Robbing God's riches (3:7-12);
- Reviling God's grace (3:13-15).

If God brings such a rebuke to these leaders, we need to pay attention to God's standards for leaders. In chapter 2 of Malachi, the Lord contrasts true and false priests. What are the qualities of a leader who is failing to lead God's people in the right way?

A Failure to Hear God's Voice (2:1-2)

The minister must hear and take to heart what God says in his Word.

Malachi 2:1-2 | And now, O priests, this command is for you. If you will not listen... then I will send the curse upon you and I will curse your blessings. Indeed, I have already cursed them, because you do not lay it to heart" (2:1-2).

Malachi says there are serious consequences for the priests who have God's Word, but do not take his words seriously. "If you will not listen..." (2:2). The leaders in Judah were not listening to God's voice. We all have this danger as well. We may be so familiar with the science of parsing Scripture, that we miss the heart of Scripture: to know the Author! It is a constant struggle for teachers and pastors in the church of Jesus to have to swim through the minutia of facts and details of context (which are surely necessary) and still hear the Author of the Scriptures. Our flesh is hungry for curious details, but our spirit is hungry for communion with the living God. There is always a battle coming to Scripture. Do we really want to hear God's voice, or are we becoming satisfied with the information alone? There is a fine line but a vast chasm at the same time.

Malachi says the minister of the Word is "the messenger of the Lord of hosts" (2:7). There is a difference between a lecture on the meaning of ancient texts and a message from the Lord of hosts, the Almighty God of the universe. God has appointed preachers in the church not simply to lead discussions, not simply to explain problems, not simply analyze texts, but to herald an eternal, transforming message to his people. And you can't herald what you don't hear. One laymen from First Baptist Church of Dallas, where W.A. Criswell was the pastor said, "Pastor, we know what the editorialists say, and we know what the commentators say, and we know what the economists and politicians say. What we want to know from you is, *Does God have anything to say?"*[41] What a curse it is to know the Scripture but not actually hear from God. There is no greater curse. That's like having an apple orchard, and not being able to eat apples. It is possible to know the Scriptures without hearing the convicting voice of God.

A Failure to Live for the Glory of God (2:2a)

Malachi says, we are to take it to heart to bring attention and honor to God's name. If we fail, our ministries are cursed and worthless. All blessing comes from giving God his honor and due. If we do not, our ministry cannot succeed, no matter how gifted or bright we may be.

Malachi 2:2a | If you will not take it to heart to give honor to my name, says the Lord of hosts, then I will send the curse upon you and I will curse your blessings.

To bring honor and glory to God in our lives and ministries, we must give credit to whom credit is due. "Unless the Lord builds the house, those who build it labor in vain" (Psa 127:1a). Ministers are to live in the reality that "Every good gift and every perfect gift is from above, coming down from the Father of lights" (Jas 1:17). "Not to us, O LORD, not to us, but to your name give glory, for the sake of your steadfast love and your faithfulness!" (Psa 115:1). We are to live in a way that gives all the credit for our lives to God. The issue is not merely whether the glory of God is a theme of the minister's teaching, but whether in

---

[41] W.A. Criswell, quoted by Piper. Sermon, "The Curse of Priestly Failure" from Malachi 2.

fact he is living in public and in private in a way that truly gives all the attention and praise to God in his life.

Listen to John Piper on this theme: "The congregation must ask, Is the glory of God not only a part of the Pastor's theology but also the passion of his soul? Does the glory of God come before the approval and praise of his people? Does it come before professional advancement? Does it come before financial reward and material comfort? Does he come back to it again and again, like the needle of a compass toward the magnet of truth, or like a weather vane in a heavenward wind? Does it come out in private as well as in public, in praying as well as preaching, in playing as well as studying?" [42]

We could ask this question in a number of ways: Is your life and the life of the pastors, elders, deacons, and other leaders man-centered or God-centered? Why is this so important? Malachi tells us. Man-centered ministries are cursed by God. That's the point. For God's blessing, we must give all glory and honor to the Lord who gave us all good things. If we fail in this, we fail in everything.

A Failure to Shepherd the People of God (2:8)

One of the main callings of a shepherd is to feed the flock of God (1 Pet 5:1-4). This is not merely teaching the Word, but also visiting the flock, getting to know them, and helping them apply the Word to their lives and the lives of their children. This is something the priests of Malachi's day failed in.

Malachi 2:8 | But you have turned aside from the way. You have caused many to stumble by your instruction. You have corrupted the covenant of Levi, says the Lord of hosts.

The priests were not living out the Word of God or giving a godly example for God's people. A minister's life must be touched by the Word of God first before he ever endeavors to teach it. Instead, the priests of Malachi's day had "turned aside from the way." They knew the Word, but were disregarding the Word and the pangs of their consciences. C. H. Spurgeon said, "Whatever 'call' a man may pretend to have, if he has not been called to holiness, he certainly has not been

---

[42] Piper, ibid.

called to the ministry."[43] Instead of pointing the sheep in the right direction, they "caused many to stumble" by their teaching. Many ministers today essentially teach "sin management" instead of true holiness. They teach psychology instead of biblical repentance. They teach "easy believism" instead of authentic conversion. No meaningful change can occur in anyone's life without the miraculous power of regeneration by the Holy Spirit. The priest neglected to teach this, perhaps because they were lost and unregenerate themselves. As a result, they "corrupted the covenant of Levi." This is language that comes from Exodus 32 reflecting the golden calf incident when the people were having a pagan festival as Moses came down Mount Sinai with the Ten Commandments. There Moses called the sons of Levi (the priests) together and asked, "Who is on the Lord's side? Come to me" (Exo 32:26). Those who joined Moses lived. The rest were executed. The priests were to be waiting on the Lord for his law. They were to be teachers and ministers who applied God's law to his people. Instead, they were leading the people in lasciviousness and sexual sin.

I was shocked recently when I heard the statistics of pastors and leaders of the church who view online pornography. "Fifty-one percent of pastors say pornography is a possible temptation. Nearly 20% of the calls received on Focus on the Family's Pastoral Care Line are for help with issues such as pornography and compulsive sexual behavior. And of the 1,351 pastors that Rick Warren's website, Pastors.com, surveyed on porn use, 54% said they had viewed internet pornography within the last year and 30% of those had visited within the last 30 days."[44] My wife and I have prayed since we were sixteen years old, that before we ever were to compromise in any way that would bring dishonor to the Lord, God would kill us. That ought to be our prayer. Without moral integrity a pastor or elder cannot effectively shepherd God's flock but will instead lead them astray, as in Malachi's day. And yet, it is true that we all are tempted with sin and capable of straying from the Lord. If you are currently looking at pornography, there is hope and there is

---

[43] Charles Haddon Spurgeon. *Lectures to My Students* (New York: Harper Collins, 2010), 5.

[44] Bo Lane, "How Many Pastors Are Addicted to Porn? The Stats are Surprising," March 25, 2014. From expastors.com.

help. But if you are a ministry leader of any kind, and you have com-
promised your integrity, you have to stop living a double life. You need
to step away and get help.

For a positive example, Peter instructs us as to how elders are to
shepherd the flock. "So I exhort the elders among you, as a fellow elder
and a witness of the sufferings of Christ, as well as a partaker in the
glory that is going to be revealed: shepherd the flock of God that is
among you, exercising oversight, not under compulsion, but willingly,
as God would have you; not for shameful gain, but eagerly; not domineering over those in your charge, but being examples to the flock. And
when the chief Shepherd appears, you will receive the unfading crown
of glory" (1 Pet 1:1-4).

The elders of the church are to be involved in the lives of the people. I want to share some notes from this past week's pastoral staff
meeting. "A goal for this year is pastoral visits to each of the 86 house-
holds at Living Hope Bible Church. What is pastoral visitation? It's a
meeting between a pastor and a church member (and their family) with
goal of determining the spiritual state of everyone in the home and to
help them in their walk with Christ through encouragement, edification, exhortation, or correction. We will also come with teaching helps
such as a Bible catechism, book recommendations (parenting & marriage, spiritual disciplines, etc.)."

If the shepherds of the church neglect the sheep, they have failed
in their calling. Sadly, there is an epidemic of wandering and lost sheep
in our congregations today, and the blame lies directly on the shoulders
of ministers who at best have lacked proper training and accountabil-
ity, and who at worst are lazy, neglectful, and even immoral. May God
spare his church from such false shepherds. Jesus says to false shepherds on Judgment Day, "Not everyone who says to me, 'Lord, Lord,'
will enter the kingdom of heaven, but the one who does the will of my
Father who is in heaven. On that day many will say to me, 'Lord, Lord,
did we not prophesy in your name, and cast out demons in your name,
and do many mighty works in your name?' And then will I declare to
them, 'I never knew you; depart from me, you workers of lawlessness'"
(Mt 7:21-23).

A Failure to Teach the Word without Partiality (2:9)

Partiality and favoritism were shown in Malachi's day by the priests teaching and preaching what people with money wanted to hear.

Malachi 2:8b-9 | You have corrupted the covenant of Levi, says the Lord of hosts, and so I make you despised and abased before all the people, inasmuch as you do not keep my ways but show partiality in your instruction.

Priests were treating the Word of God the same way they were treating the sacrifices of God. You give God the sacrifices that will leave you with the most money. And you give the people the teaching that will bring in the most money.

John Piper describes this mindset: "You play to your audience. You say what 'Daddy Warbucks' wants to hear. You step on no toes. You say, 'Peace! Peace!' when there is no peace.' Or to put it the way Micah 3:11 puts it, 'The heads of Jerusalem give judgment for a bribe, its priests teach for hire, its prophets divine for money.' When the glory of God no longer satisfies the heart of a preacher, then he will seek his satisfaction elsewhere. And I don't mean by leaving his pulpit; but just by using the Word of God to get gain."[45]

Pastors and elders must teach God's Word without partiality, regarding all equally in need of hearing the whole counsel of God. We ought to disregard position, no matter how high, for there is no position higher than God and his Word. All must surrender and be subject to the one who judges our souls.

A Failure to Lead with Integrity (2:8)

Malachi 2:8 | You have caused many to stumble by your instruction. You have corrupted the covenant of Levi, says the Lord of hosts.

Are the sins of teachers and leaders more grievous than the sins of others? Yes, they are. Not necessarily because the sin in and of itself is worse, but because its evil is compounded by the weight of public responsibility that should have restrained it. It is more grievous for the priests to sin than for the people to sin, because when the priests sin,

---

[45] Piper. Sermon, "The Curse of Priestly Failure" from Malachi 2.

they cause many to stumble. "To whom much is given, much will be required" (Lk 12:48).

David Neff wrote in an article in Christianity Today: "The leader who philanders has broken a trust placed in him by a wide community—trust in his vision, reliability, wisdom, and veracity. And the essence of leadership is that trust. So a leader who violates trust in a fundamental and public manner is ipso facto no longer a leader."[46]

True leadership rests on the foundation of personal integrity. This does not call for perfection, but blamelessness. Blamelessness is not perfection, but an openness about the sins the leader struggles with and a general consistency and faithfulness in living righteously.

THE PRICE FOR FAILED LEADERSHIP (2:2-3)

What happens when leadership fails by constantly violating his conscience? In the New Testament, St. Paul warns that we should be "holding faith and a good conscience. By rejecting this, some have made shipwreck of their faith" (1 Tim 1:19). What does a minister lose when he is shipwrecked? God tells us through Malachi.

Loss of Favor with God

Malachi 2:2a | I will send a curse upon you.

Cursing and hatred convey rejection. "Many are called but few are chosen." This is a revelation that the leaders and believers in name only. The result of unrepentance (signified by boredom and weariness) is a destructive curse (2:2), probably having in mind those curses promised for those guilty of breach of covenant in Deuteronomy 28:15–68.[47] Christ himself warns that a multitude of ministers will come before him on that day, and despite their preaching and miracles performed, he will command them "Depart from me... I never knew you" (Mt 7:21-23).

Loss of Blessing

The Lord goes on to curse the priests.

Malachi 2:2b | I will curse your blessings.

---

[46] David Neff. *Are All Sins Created Equal?* (Wheaton: Christianity Today. Nov. 20, 1987), 20

[47] Baker. *Malachi*, 241.

In other words, the ministry of the Word that was meant to bring life will instead kill. Those who sin in the light will be hardened by the light. The puritans used to say, "The same sun that softens the wax hardens the clay." So it is that ministers who should be softened by the Word will harden their consciences to it because they do not practice it.

Loss of Prosperity

Malachi 2:3a | I will rebuke your offspring" (2:3a).

This likely refers to children and crops. He will hold them back from fertility and prosperity. I have seen shipwrecked ministers lose everything they've worked for their whole lives in just one day. There are those who have studied the ancient languages, achieved great knowledge through graduate and post graduate degrees harden their conscience, and as a result resign from the church never to shepherd again. They lose their reputation, their trustworthiness, and their livelihood all at once. How devastating it is to think of a shipwrecked minister.

Loss of Reputation

Malachi 2:3b | I will... spread dung on your faces, the dung of your offerings.

A shipwrecked shepherd's ability to minister is as worthless as the dung of animal sacrifices. The interpretation and application is in 2:9, "I make you despised and abased before all the people." God will expose hypocritical ministers as the frauds they are. Every minister should tremble before the Lord and ask him to do whatever it takes for him to remain pure, sincere, holy, humble, and childlike before the Lord and the Lord's people.

THE PROOFS OF GODLY LEADERSHIP (2:4-7)

Here we find the prototype of true minister. This prototype is so sacred that when the people of Israel violated this prototype (with Aaron leading them), the Lord commanded Moses to execute 3000 who were worshipping the Egyptian bull god (Exo 32:15-29). Aaron made excuses. He said to Moses: "I told them, 'Whoever has gold jewelry, take it off.' When they brought it to me, I simply threw it into the fire—

and out came this calf!" (Exo 32:24, NLT). This is the exact opposite of what the priests ought to be. Instead of excuse making and idolatrous, they should be faithful to God in their office. Malachi reminds us what God's covenant with the Levitical priests was by giving us the original prototype of the priest.

The prototype of the priest in Malachi 2:4-7 is also the model for God's New Testament minister.[48] The prophet names five marks of a true minister: character, clarity, consistency, courage, and conversions (spiritual fruit). Let us also remember that this is also a prototype for every New Testament believer since the Lord said, "...you are a chosen race, a royal priesthood, a holy nation, a people for his own possession, that you may proclaim the excellencies of him who called you out of darkness into his marvelous light" (1 Pet 2:9).

Character: Faithful Walk with God

A true minister and true believer first has godly character based on a right relationship with God.

Malachi 2:4-5 | So shall you know that I have sent this command to you, that my covenant with Levi may stand, says the Lord of hosts. My covenant with him was one of life and peace, and I gave them to him. It was a covenant of fear, and he feared me. He stood in awe of my name.

Levi feared the Lord. He kept the covenant with God out of a re-newed and regenerated heart. Though he deserved death and destruc-tion, God gave him (and us) "life and peace." St. Anselm prayed for the love every Christian leader ought to have: "O Lord our God, grant us grace to desire Thee with our whole heart; that, so desiring, we may seek, and seeking find Thee; and so finding Thee may love Thee; and in loving Thee, may hate those sins from which Thou hast redeemed us."

A godly minister may or may not be supremely gifted or be abounding in intellect, but above all, he must have a godly character. We read of Levi: "He feared me. He stood in awe of my name." The first

---

[48]The categorization and explanation of these traits are primarily adapted from John Piper. *The Glory of Priestly Success* (Minneapolis, MN: Desiring God, November 15, 1987) https://www.desiringgod.org/messages/the-glory-of-priestly-success; and Mark Driscoll. *Will You Listen?* (Seattle: Mars Hill Church Archive, December 8, 2013), http://marshill.se/marshill/media/malachi-living-for-a-legacy/will-you-listen.

priority of any Christian leader ought to be: "What does my life say about the Lord? How can I reflect the character of Christ in my heart and life?" We'd say he lived *Coram Deo*, or "in the face of God." Malachi is a man of character as well. He fears God, and he loves people. They can't look at him and say, "You don't know the Lord. You don't walk with the Lord. You're no better than us." No, they can't throw any of that at Malachi because he wasn't a perfect man, but he was a man of character.

We need to be careful. Our Lord says that many leaders who seem to have good character are actually shallow in character and are actually unconverted and lost. "Not everyone who says to me, 'Lord, Lord,' will enter the kingdom of heaven, but the one who does the will of my Father who is in heaven. On that day many will say to me, 'Lord, Lord, did we not prophesy in your name, and cast out demons in your name, and do many mighty works in your name?' And then will I declare to them, 'I never knew you; depart from me, you workers of lawlessness'" (Mt 7:21-23).

A minister's highest calling is not primarily gifting or knowledge, but character. A person may be supremely gifted and knowledgeable about the Word of God, but if they have bad character they cannot be used of God in any meaningful way. Someone said, "You can borrow brains, but you cannot borrow character." Without character, the messenger of God has no integrity and therefore, no credibility. Charles Spurgeon said, "Whatever 'call' a man may pretend to have, if he has not been called to holiness, he certainly has not been called to the ministry."[49] A Christian leader's first responsibility is not teaching the Word to others, but feeding on the Word himself. Without that hunger for holiness the man or woman of God will lack humility. "God opposes the proud but gives grace to the humble" (Jas 4:6).

Clarity: Faithful Instruction with the Word

The minister should have a personal commitment by the ministry of God's Word.

Malachi 2:6a | True instruction was in his mouth, and no wrong was found on his lips.

---

[49] Charles Spurgeon. *Lectures to My Students* (Peabody, MA: Hendrickson Publishers, 2010), 6.

The lips of the messenger is the public reservoir for the church. We are not merely to insist on right doctrine but upon changed lives. There's nothing worse than someone who opens the Scriptures and fog comes out. A minister must have clarity in his doctrine and in his life. Paul's exhortation to Timothy is needful for us to hear today: "Keep a close watch on yourself and on the teaching. Persist in this, for by so doing you will save both yourself and your hearers" (1 Tim 4:16).

The clarity a minister must have is in the proclamation of the Gospel. There's one God. He made you. You sinned against him. He loves you, so he sent his Son Jesus Christ to save you. Jesus lived without sin and died on the cross in your place for your sins. Three days later, he arose from death. "Death is dead, love has won, Christ has conquered!"[50] He's ascended, seated in heaven right now, and he's coming again to judge the living and the dead. The bottom line is, you've got two options: You close your ears, you harden your heart, you live in your sin, you stand before him, and you spend forever in the conscious, eternal torments of hell. Or you open your ears, you soften your heart, you confess your sins, you receive him as Lord and Savior, you close your eyes in death, and you awaken to see him face-to-face and to be with him forever in heaven. This is clarity.

For the Christian leader, we must never back away from clarity. Frustration rises watching many a media interview, and the interviewer asks with millions watching, "Is Jesus the only way to heaven?" Sadly, the common response is, "Well, there are various perspectives, and I don't want to judge anyone." We've all seen that interview, and we are shouting at the television: "Say yes! Say yes! Come on!" Are you clear with your presentation of the truth? Are you clear in presenting the Gospel and the exclusivity of Jesus?

Consistency: Godliness in Daily Living

The minister should be marked by godly character and progress in his spiritual life.

Malachi 2:6b | He walked with me in peace and uprightness.

---

[50] Keith Getty and Stuart Townsend. "See What a Morning," *In Christ Alone* (Brentwood, TN: Thank You Music, 2003).

Success is not the measure of one's life. Success for the true minister is to teach the whole message of God. We need to have godly character and submissive obedience which brings consistency in the Christian life. We read of Levi, "He walked with me in peace and righteousness." When the Bible uses the language of "walk," this is a lifestyle, walking with God. It's not like, "Well, he walked with me one season, and then he walked with his mistress when his wife wasn't looking, and then he walked over to the church and embezzled some money, and then walked away from the ministry because he just didn't feel like doing it anymore, and then walked back in and asked for his job." That's not a good and consistent walk. God says of the godly minister: "He walked with me." One commentator calls this "long obedience in the same direction."[51] A true teacher of God's Word can't have a reverse gear. Imposters are inconsistent. They say, "I love Jesus, and now I don't, and I'm walking with Jesus, and now I'm not." A true minister is consistently, though not perfectly, moving forward.

It is easy to get enamored by what is new and get bored with what is eternal. The key is to be consistent over time. Keep meditating. Keep studying. Keep persevering. Keep your eyes on Christ! I've had people come up and say, "Pastor Matt, what you told us today—we already knew that." Well, maybe you needed to hear it again. That's why sometimes the Bible says things more than once, or maybe somebody just showed up and they never heard it. The message of the Bible is like a rhythm. Sound doctrine is proclaimed over and over again. The Gospel does not need editing. It needs proclaiming. Consistency.

Courage: Speaking for Convictions

The minister should also be marked by godly convictions and compassion for others. It is said of Levi:

Malachi 2:6c | I He turned many from iniquity [lawlessness].

We have to be able to speak up for biblical convictions. Levi turned many from living in the lawlessness of the surrounding nations or of one's own heart. This takes courage. What this means is that most doctrinal problems are actually moral or ethical problems, historically, even in our own day.

---

[51] Eugene H. Peterson. *A Long Obedience in the Same Direction: Discipleship in an Instant Society* (Downers Grove, IL: IVP Books, 2000).

People want to practice some sort of behavior that God forbids. All of a sudden they will couch it as theologically problematic, and then they teach the exact opposite of what it says, giving you many reasons why the Bible does not say what it obviously says. We see it in our day of post-modern logic, where people are happy to believe contradictory things. We have to stand up and cry out from the rooftops the truth and be counter-cultural. You might say, "that's mean." No, that's compassionate. If there is a disease going around, and I say, "You have the disease!" – that's not rude. That's not mean. That's compassionate, especially if I have the cure, and I'm willing to administer it.

Conversions: Transformation of People

The true minister will have a godly influence upon those under his call.

Malachi 2:7 | For the lips of a priest should guard knowledge, and people should seek instruction from his mouth, for he is the messenger of the Lord of hosts.

God has given the godly minister a great trust. The minister has the awesome privilege of "guarding knowledge." The minister is not to edit the message of the Word, but to faithfully speak it into the lives of people. The message of the Word doesn't need improvement, it needs guarding. People are reached for Christ, and they are transformed into his image by the faithful proclamation of God's Word. The fruit of a godly minister is the conversion and transformation of souls by the faithful exposition of the Word of God. Here we find the original prototype of the minister's true calling: "people should seek instruction from his mouth." We see the contrast between the success portrayed in verses 5–7 and the failures of the priests in Malachi's day.

This last contrast may be the clearest of all. "He turned many from iniquity" (2:6) is just the opposite of the second phrase in verse 8:

Malachi 2:8a | But you have turned aside from the way. You have caused many to stumble by your instruction.

The minister's preaching can destroy, and the ministry can save. When your ministry is rooted in the glory of God and your teaching is strong with the Word of God and your life displays the righteousness of God, then the fruit of your life is going to be the salvation of sinners by the grace of God.

The minister of God will give an account to almighty God. In the case of anyone who mishandles God's Word, there is a severe consequence:

Malachi 2:8b-9 | You have corrupted the covenant of Levi, says the Lord of hosts, and so I make you despised and abased before all the people, inasmuch as you do not keep my ways but show partiality in your instruction.

The way of the transgressor is hard. There will be eternal shame and disgrace for the pastoral hypocrite. Our Lord reminds us that "many will come" to him on Judgment Day and claim to know Christ merely because they have handled his Word, performed miracles, and cast our demons. Jesus says to a multitude of false ministers on that day, "Depart from me, I never knew you" (Mt 7:21-23).

Conclusion

The true minister of God sacrifices his life to lead God's flock. If we say we love God, then we will be seeking a church with a true minister who invests his life into God's people. It is a tragedy that so many attend churches with lukewarm and often barebones preaching and teaching. Many people are consumers looking for a church that will bend and edit the message to conform to worldly expectations. Sadly, there are many church members that do not know the ministers of their church in any personal way. If you love the Lord, you will seek to be shepherded by true ministers who will sacrifice their lives for you.

Would you commit yourself to pray every day that the glory of God and the Word of God and the righteousness of God would so fill your minister and your church that people would turn away from sin, and receive the salvation of Jesus Christ in your church and in your neighborhood? Would you pray that the churches in your city or town will faithfully proclaim and apply the Scriptures that lives may be transformed?

4 | MALACHI 2:10-16

IF YOU LOVE ME, LOVE YOUR SPOUSE

'For I hate divorce!' says the Lord, the God of Israel. 'To divorce your wife is to overwhelm her with cruelty,' says the Lord of Heaven's Armies. 'So guard your heart;
do not be unfaithful to your wife.'
MALACHI 2:16 (NLT)

God's plan of redemption is mirrored in marriage. We make a promise to love one another "for better or for worse, for richer or poorer, in sickness and in health, till death do we part." God's love story is deeper and wider than our earthly romances. Before the foundation of the world he loved us. That's really what this portion of Scripture is all about. We as the Body of Christ on this earth are to reflect the love of God in our lives and in marriage. We are to reflect God's covenant of redemption in our covenants on earth.

Three covenants are mentioned in our text: God's covenant to Abraham in Genesis 12 and 15, his covenant with Moses in Exodus 20, and the covenant he gives to husband and wife in marriage. If we are truly faithful and genuine Christians, God will give us the grace to be faithful to these covenants. The priests of Malachi's day were not being faithful to these covenants.

Once a person breaks his commitment to God, his relationships with human beings also suffer. God's commandments constitute the only sufficient basis for a meaningful and authoritative system of ethics, and in turn, one's obedience to these commandments is the only proper basis for being faithful and ethical in one's personal relationships. One who is not faithful to God may still appear to be faithful to his wife or his friends, but without faithfulness to God as the context and background, all his apparently faithful actions are superficial, and ultimately sinful.[52]

DON'T BREAK MY COVENANT OF GRACE (2:10)
The Abrahamic Covenant
Malachi does not first begin with the problem of divorce and broken homes. He begins where we all ought to begin: in our relationship and covenant with God.

Malachi 2:10 | Have we not all one Father? Has not one God created us? Why then are we faithless to one another, profaning the covenant of our fathers?

The first question hearkens back to God's covenant with Abraham in Genesis 12, 15 and 17. "Have we not all one Father?" Aren't we people of faith? Do we not believe in the "one God" who created us? Are we not distinct from the nations who worship many gods?

Why don't we stay strong in the faith of Abraham? Why are we profaning the covenant of our fathers, Abraham, Isaac, and Jacob? Here is a reference to the covenant God made with Abraham, the father of the Israelite people (Isa 51:2; *cf* Mt 3:9).[53] To apply it in modern terms, we might say – your marriage problems are not first and foremost about your marriage. Your marriage problems are indicative of a much deeper problem. You are not committed to Christ as you ought to be. Don't start with the problems you have with your spouse. Your spouse is not your savior. Start with the real problem. You are not relying on the covenant you have with Jesus who is the only true Savior.

God's covenants in the Old Testament were covenants of grace. Consider the Abrahamic Covenant in Genesis 15:1-6 (cf Gen 12, 17), "After these things the word of the Lord came to Abram in a vision: 'Fear not, Abram, I am your shield; your reward shall be very great.' But

[52] Vincent Cheung. *Commentary on Malachi* (Morrisville, NC: Lulu Publishing, 2014), Kindle Locations 1167-1170.
[53] Baker, *Malachi*, 251.

Abram said, 'O Lord God, what will you give me, for I continue child-less, and the heir of my house is Eliezer of Damascus?' And Abram said, 'Behold, you have given me no offspring, and a member of my house-hold will be my heir.' And behold, the word of the Lord came to him: 'This man shall not be your heir; your very own son shall be your heir.' And he brought him outside and said, 'Look toward heaven, and num-ber the stars, if you are able to number them.' Then he said to him, 'So shall your offspring be.' And he believed the Lord, and he counted it to him as righteousness."

Here we have the Old Testament way of salvation – the only way – by grace through faith. "For by grace you have been saved through faith. And this is not your own doing; it is the gift of God, not a result of works, so that no one may boast" (Eph 2:8-9; cf Rom 4:3; Gal 3:6).

God's Grace in the Old Testament

This theme is repeated throughout the Bible, most notably in Hab-akkuk, and it is quoted again in Romans 1:16-17, "For I am not ashamed of the gospel, for it is the power of God for salvation to everyone who believes, to the Jew first and also to the Greek. For in it the righteous-ness of God is revealed from faith for faith, as it is written, 'The right-eous shall live by faith.'" St. Paul explains that the concept of justifica-tion by grace through faith is an Old Testament concept. The Law and the Prophets (the 39 books of the Old Testament) bear witness that grace, not the Law of Moses, has always justified the believer. "But now the righteousness of God has been manifested apart from the law, alt-hough the Law and the Prophets bear witness to it—the righteousness of God through faith in Jesus Christ for all who believe. For there is no distinction: for all have sinned and fall short of the glory of God, and are justified by his grace as a gift, through the redemption that is in Christ Jesus, whom God put forward as a propitiation by his blood, to be received by faith. This was to show God's righteousness, because in his divine forbearance he had passed over former sins. It was to show his righteousness at the present time, so that he might be just and the justifier of the one who has faith in Jesus" (Rom 3:21-26). When God appeared to Moses he declared that he was "The LORD, the LORD, a God merciful and gracious, slow to anger, and abounding in steadfast love and faithfulness" (Exo 34:6). In both Old and New Testaments, mercy and grace have always been only way to eternal life.

A Rediscovery of Grace in the Reformation

We need God's grace through faith because we have no righteousness apart from God. The phrase "a righteousness from God" was the phrase that led Martin Luther into the light of the truth that produced the Protestant Reformation. Luther confessed later that he had always hated the expression "the righteousness of God," for it suggested to him a stern judge, waiting to hurl thunderbolts of judgment down on helpless, disobedient men. Through his study of the Psalms in the year 1514 Luther learned that the righteousness of God was related to man's deliverance, not man's condemnation. Commenting on his experience years later in 1545, Luther said: "As violently as I had formerly hated the expression 'righteousness of God,' so I was now as violently compelled to embrace the new conception of grace and, for me, the expression of the Apostle really opened the Gates of Paradise."[54]

True righteousness is unearned – Martin Luther discovered for his day that justification in God's sight comes through pure grace. Yet this was nothing new. This was the message Abraham of old heard from God. The righteousness of God, then, is the key to salvation for Abraham, Martin Luther, and for us today. Those who have that unmerited righteousness by faith know the power of God in personal salvation, and they know that they are right before God because of God's grace. Before Christ, God's people looked forward to the cross. Peter says precisely this: "Concerning this salvation, the prophets who prophesied about the grace that was to be yours searched and inquired carefully, inquiring what person or time the Spirit of Christ in them was indicating when he predicted the sufferings of Christ and the subsequent glories. It was revealed to them that they were serving not themselves but you, in the things that have now been announced to you through those who preached the good news to you by the Holy Spirit sent from heaven, things into which angels long to look" (1 Pet 1:10-12).

The children of Israel in Malachi's day were to return to God's covenant of grace in Christ that we see through the whole Bible. They had thrown off grace and were living under a messy syncretistic works-based salvation. They were "profaning" the covenant of their fathers, Abraham, Isaac, and Jacob, by worshipping the idols of the nations around them. In other words, they were nominal in their faith. They

---

[54] S. Lewis Johnson. *Discovering Romans: Spiritual Revival for the Soul* (Grand Rapids, MI: Zondervan, 2014), 28.

knew the theology of Abraham, but they did not practice it. They did not understand the freedom of grace but were instead in bondage to the gods of this world.

God's Grace in National Holiness

Malachi 2:10 | Have we not all one Father?

The prophet Malachi was asking, "Are we not distinct from the nations around us? We are not tossed about by many gods, but we serve one faithful God of grace." God had protected them from amalgamating into the other nations by his manifest presence among them in the Tabernacle and the Temple. They were distinct from the other nations because of the grace of God alone. As many times as they had turned to idolatry, the Lord had preserved them with his presence.

God's Grace in Personal Holiness

How about you? Are you living in the freedom of Christ's grace and love? The love we were made for cannot ultimately be found in marriage, money or even church. We need to look to the love of God in Christ. "I have always loved you" (1:2, NLT). God said it to Israel, and he says it to you. "Christ's love compels us" (2 Cor 5:14, HCSB). No longer are we in bondage to the false saviors of this world like money, sex or fame, but "the joy of the Lord is your strength" (Neh 8:10). It's not our love for God but his love for us that compels us. St. Augustine clarifies this idea and gives us deep encouragement: "Beware of despairing about yourself; you are commanded to place your trust in God, and not in yourself."[55] No longer are we in bondage to the guilt of sin. "Now the law came in to increase the trespass, but where sin increased, grace abounded all the more, so that, as sin reigned in death, grace also might reign through righteousness leading to eternal life through Jesus Christ our Lord. What shall we say then? Are we to continue in sin that grace may abound? By no means! How can we who died to sin still live in it?" (Rom 5:20-6:2).

The children of Israel in Malachi's day were just giving up and giving in to paganism – turning the gifts of God into gods. As Christians, if we try and compartmentalize our problems (such as marriage or finances or children, etc.), we miss the only pathway to change. Every

---

[55] K. W. Osbeck, *Amazing Grace: 366 Inspiring Hymn Stories for Daily Devotions* (Grand Rapids, MI: Kregel Publications, 1996), 340.

problem we face always has at its root a failure to seek the living God. "Seek first the kingdom of God and his righteousness, and all these things will be added to you" (Mt 6:33). We need to rediscover the love of God in the same way Abraham discovered it.

Abraham's covenant of grace should have amazed the people of Malachi's day. They should have trusted God's love, but instead they doubted it. That seed of doubt ruined not only their relationship with God but had a devastating effect on their family. How sad it is that God gave his people a message of love through Malachi, but because of their doubt they missed it, and their lives were destroyed, beginning with their marriages. We must never forget, our relationship with the Lord is the sure foundation of all of life. Without that divine footing, we can be sure that marriage, family, and the very fabric of Judeo-Christian society is at risk.

DON'T BREAK MY COVENANT OF LOVE (2:11-12)
The Law Covenant at Sinai

Malachi 2:11-12 | Judah has been faithless, and abomination has been committed in Israel and in Jerusalem. For Judah has profaned the sanctuary of the Lord, which he loves, and has married the daughter of a foreign god. May the Lord cut off from the tents of Jacob any descendant of the man who does this, who brings an offering to the Lord of hosts!

Malachi here deals with the ramifications of Israel's unfaithfulness to God in breaking the covenant at Sinai which was to love God and reverence him as the one true and living God. That covenant summarized in Exodus 20 forbade God's people from worshipping other gods. The prophet makes the charge that God's people committed "an abomination" by having "married the daughter of a foreign god." The people of Judah always loved God's sanctuary in the Temple and the worship, but now having forsaken the Lord, the home disintegrates. Without a true love for God, the home is in danger. It is true today, and it was true in Malachi's day. Our relationship with God affects all our other relationships, especially marriage. Spiritual infidelity has a tragic effect on marriage. If we do not love God, we will not properly love our spouse.

The Law of Moses is a law of love. Our Lord summarizes the entire law as a covenant of love: "You shall love the Lord your God with all your heart and with all your soul and with all your mind. This is the great and first commandment. And a second is like it: You shall love your neighbor as yourself. On these two commandments depend all the Law and the Prophets" (Mt 22:37-40).

Interfaith Marriages Forbidden

To be clear, Malachi was not forbidding marrying someone outside of Israel. Baldwin argues that the issue is not interracial marriages, but interfaith marriages. She writes: "There was no objection on racial grounds to intermarriage. A mixed multitude went out of Egypt with the Israelites (Exo 12:38), but by submitting to circumcision and keeping the Passover they committed themselves to the God of Israel (Exo 12:48; Num 9:14). Boaz married Ruth the Moabitess, but she had forsaken Chemosh for Israel's God."[56]

Sinai's Law-Covenant Forbids Loving Idols

Israel's covenant relationship with God meant he was their God and they were his people. To safeguard that relationship God commanded them not to intermarry with the surrounding nations who worshipped other gods (Deut 7:3–4). This forbidden practice of idol worship had now become so widespread that the prophet could legitimately say that the whole nation of Judah had 'profaned' the Lord's institution. What was Malachi saying? Simply this: the broken marriages of the nation were symptomatic of a deeper problem. The high divorce rate indicated hearts that were divorced from God. The men were "treating their marriages so casually" because of their casual attitude toward the Lord and his worship.[57] The men dissolved their marriages for unlawful pagan women because their hearts were far from God, and they loved the sensuality and worldly pleasure of pagan worship. The men of Israel married women who led them into idolatry. This is the essence of God's Law-covenant at Sinai. God want his people – husbands and wives, children – to worship him alone. Who you marry often uncovers what you really want in your heart. Someone who truly loves Christ will marry a worshipper of Christ. The men of Israel were not only divorcing their wives, but they were marrying foreign women who would lead the men of Israel into idolatry.

---

[56] Baldwin, *Malachi*, 240–241.
[57] Ellsworth, 53-54.

The modern equivalent to a mixed marriage is a believer marrying an unbeliever. The apostle Paul pointedly says: "Do not be unequally yoked together with unbelievers. For what fellowship has righteousness with lawlessness? And what communion has light with darkness? And what accord has Christ with Belial? Or what part has a believer with an unbeliever? And what agreement has the temple of God with idols? For you are the temple of the living God. As God has said: 'I will dwell in them and walk among them. I will be their God, and they shall be my people'" (2 Cor 6:14–16).

A yoke is a harness for an animal plow. If you have two oxen, they go in the same direction, but if you have an ox and a donkey, the donkey will refuse to plow straight. God designed marriage to be optimized when both husband and wife have a strong walk with the living God and they are going in the same direction. If you are not both moving each other forward to the Lord, there is an almost certain likelihood that the person who does not know Christ will move the marriage toward the world. If you are single, make your choice of a mate wisely.

DON'T BREAK MY COVENANT OF MARRIAGE (2:13-16a)
The Marriage Covenant

Malachi 2:13-16 | And this second thing you do. You cover the Lord's altar with tears, with weeping and groaning because he no longer regards the offering or accepts it with favor from your hand. But you say, 'Why does he not?' Because the Lord was witness between you and the wife of your youth, to whom you have been faithless, though she is your companion and your wife by covenant. Did he not make them one, with a portion of the Spirit in their union? And what was the one God seeking? Godly offspring. So guard yourselves in your spirit, and let none of you be faithless to the wife of your youth. 'For the man who does not love his wife but divorces her, says the Lord, the God of Israel, covers his garment with violence, says the Lord of hosts. So guard yourselves in your spirit, and do not be faithless.'

Perhaps a better translation of verse 16 is in the New Living Translation: "'For I hate divorce!' says the Lord, the God of Israel. 'To divorce your wife is to overwhelm her with cruelty,' says the Lord of Heaven's Armies. 'So guard your heart; do not be unfaithful to your wife.'"

As we have noted, the men of Israel were divorcing their wives in exchange for sensual pagan women and practices. This blatant disregard for their marriage vows prompted God to say that he hates divorce (2:16). It violates his ideal of oneness (2:10, 15; Gen 2:24). To say God hates divorce is to say that he hates everything that leads up to divorce, which means he also hates all our failures to work towards real companionship and oneness in marriage. We may be inclined to think that what goes on in our homes doesn't have any bearing on the rest of life, but it does. Here in Malachi's day we find men going to meet the Lord at the Temple, and the Lord points them back to their homes. Family life colors and influences every other part of life.[58]

Your Marriage Reflects Your Walk with God

Your relationships in your home are connected to your relationship with God. Consider 1 Peter 3:7, "Likewise, husbands, live with your wives in an understanding way, showing honor to the woman as the weaker vessel, since they are heirs with you of the grace of life, so that your prayers may not be hindered." If your relationship with your spouse is not right, then your relationship with God is hindered. God has called us to love him by loving others, especially those in our own household.

Marriage is not simply a social arrangement constructed by men. It is the design of God himself (Gen 2:21–24). Malachi makes it clear that God not only designed marriage, but he also designed it in a certain way. He calls attention to the fact that at the beginning God created only one companion for Adam. He could, of course, have created many women. Malachi says God had "a remnant of the Spirit." In other words, God's creative acts in no way diminished his power or ability. He still had plenty of power after he created to create more. After he took Eve from Adam's side, God's power was in no way depleted or expended. He could have made more wives for Adam. In making Eve alone, then, the Lord was making it plain that his design for marriage was for a man to have one wife.[59]

---

[58] Ibid., 54-55.
[59] Ibid., 56.

Your Marriage Has a Major Effect on Your Children

Another harmful effect of this faithless dealing had to do with the children involved. Why did God want his people to be faithful to their marriages? Malachi's answer is still relevant today: "He seeks godly offspring" (2:15). "Only when both parents remain faithful to their marriage vows can the children be given the security which provides the basis for godly living. The family was intended to be the school in which God's way of life was practiced and learned."[60]

"He is seeking godly offspring. He is looking for our children to become disciples. Of course, there is no guarantee that children of Christian parents will automatically embrace the faith of their parents... But we must realize that an unhappy Christian marriage, where the thought life (and therefore probably the words and actions) of the partners is far from perfect harmony, will be a profound obstacle to our children becoming Christians."[61]

QUESTIONS

Let me answer some hard questions about divorce and remarriage, and then consider why faithfulness in marriage is so important.

Does God Ever Permit Divorce?

There is not perfect agreement on this, but most Bible teachers agree that divorce is permitted for two reasons: unrepentant adultery and desertion by an unbeliever.

Unrepentant Adultery

Our Lord tells us in the New Testament, "Whoever divorces his wife, except for sexual immorality, and marries another, commits adultery" (Mat 19:9). The key is the interpretation of the word "sexual immorality" which is the Greek word *pornea*. All agree that it is more than just adultery, because he could have said "adultery," but it is at minimum unrepentant adultery and includes devious sexual sins and other vices. Though divorce is permitted between believers in the circumstance of adultery, it is not necessarily required. We must always remember the story of Hosea in the Bible who loves his unfaithful wife and demonstrates God's covenant faithfulness. Even when his wife

---

[60] Baldwin, 240–241.
[61] Benton, 79.

Gomer broke the marriage covenant Hosea remained married to Gomer.

Desertion by an Unbeliever

"But if the unbelieving partner separates, let it be so. In such cases the brother or sister is not enslaved. God has called you to peace" (1 Cor 7:15). Sometimes the unbeliever will desert the believer, but often it is far more complicated. Many times the unbeliever does not leave or ask for a divorce, but rendered the marriage unsafe and unlivable and therefore has deserted the marriage. Examples of unbelievers who have left the marriage would be:

- One who physically leaves and abandons the marriage
- An abuser (physically violent or sexually deviant)
- A railer (verbally abusive to the point of sociopathic behavior)

What About Unbiblical Divorce?

If remarriage in any other circumstance is adultery, what about those that have remarried without biblical grounds? What should they do? I do not think that a person who remarries against God's will, and thus commits adultery in this way, should later break the second marriage. Deuteronomy 24:1-4 forbids one who is remarried to go back and marry his first wife. This tells us that God recognizes the second marriage. In other words, the marriage should not have been covenanted in the first place, but now that it is done, it should not be undone by man. It is a real marriage. Real vows have been made and sexual union has occurred. This is now a genuine covenant of marriage and may be purified by the blood of Jesus and set apart for God. I don't think that a couple who repents and seeks God's forgiveness, receiving his cleansing, should think of their lives as ongoing adultery, even though, in the eyes of Jesus, that's how the relationship started.

What Was Jesus' Opinion of Divorce?

God hates divorce. Lifelong monogamy was God's original design of Genesis 2. The story of Jesus' opinion of divorce is told when "some Pharisees came to him to test him. They asked, 'Is it lawful for a man to divorce his wife for any and every reason?' 'Haven't you read,' he replied, 'that at the beginning the Creator 'made them male and female,' and said, 'For this reason a man will leave his father and mother and be united to his wife, and the two will become one flesh'? So they are no longer two, but one flesh. Therefore what God has joined together, let no one separate.' 'Why then,' they asked, 'did Moses command that a man give his wife a certificate of divorce and send her away?' Jesus replied, 'Moses permitted you to divorce your wives because your hearts were hard. But it was not this way from the beginning. I tell you that anyone who divorces his wife, except for sexual immorality, and marries another woman commits adultery'" (Mt 19:3-9).

This question was asked because divorce was quite prevalent in Jesus' day. Divorce was a controversial issue in Jesus' day. The Jews divorced and remarried in Jesus' day as much or more than our own culture. There were two schools of thought in Jesus' day. Rabbi Shammai taught you could only divorce if the woman was found to be immoral during the betrothal period. Rabbi Hillel, which was the prevalent view, taught that you could divorce for any reason. But Jesus went beyond both schools by saying, "anyone who divorces his wife, except for sexual immorality, and marries another woman commits adultery" (Mt 19:9). In other words, except for *pornea* – including adultery, sexual deviation, sexual abuse, etc. – a believer is never permitted to divorce. In 1 Corinthians 7, St. Paul adds abandonment as a legitimate cause for divorce. The point Jesus was making is not that it's ok to divorce. No. He was emphasizing the sacredness of marriage to the point where the disciples reaction to his teaching was: "If this is the situation between a husband and wife, it is better not to marry" (Mt 19:10). In other words, God hates divorce. If at all possible, God's people should remain married.

Jesus ends his answer to the Pharisees, with the powerful command, "Let no man separate [what God joined]" (Mt 19:6). Since it is God's joining, only God can separate, and that separation is by death. Romans 7 as well, among other places, tells us that there is only one thing that ought to separate a marriage—it is an act of God in death. God brings death to a spouse, and you are free to remarry. Romans 7:2-3, "For a married woman is bound by law to her husband while he lives, but if her husband dies she is released from the law of marriage. Accordingly, she will be called an adulteress if she lives with another man while her husband is alive. But if her husband dies, she is free from that law, and if she marries another man she is not an adulteress."

What are the Consequences of Divorce?

The prophet Malachi cried out in his day as we should herald in our day.

Malachi 2:16 | 'For I hate divorce!' says the Lord, the God of Israel. 'To divorce your wife is to overwhelm her with cruelty,' says the Lord of Heaven's Armies. 'So guard your heart; do not be unfaithful to your wife' (NLT).

From Jesus' day to our day, divorce puts a wife and possible children in the cruelest circumstances one can imagine. The financial, social, emotional and phycological toll of divorce over a lifetime is beyond comprehension.

With abandonment of divorce comes deep emotional consequences. Rejection takes hold and paralyzes the soul with rage and anger. These emotions may go on for years. There is deep grief. Divorce is like a death with no closure because there is no funeral. It's cruel because you most likely see the person that divorced you over and over again. Then there is the anxiety. What will happen to me? Our children? The children are robbed of a parent for half or more of the time. Divorce affects all of us. Many of us grew up with the bitterness of fighting and shouting in the home. Some grow up with outright abuse in the home. Our culture does not take marriage seriously. Consider that around five out of ten marriages in our culture today will end in divorce. Divorce devastates families and children. It is the cause of years of bitterness and distress. It tears children apart. Divorce brings the devastation of not having a father in your life. I was raised for many years without a father.

I am from a family that decided to divorce. My mother divorced my father after 24 years of marriage for a love affair. The love affair lasted about six weeks, and then my mother lived another six years and died at the age of 49. Each member of my family has suffered because of it. Without Christ, divorce becomes the norm for many who don't want to deal with the difficulties of marriage. "So many persons think divorce a panacea for every ill, find out, when they try it, that the remedy is worse than the disease."[62] Divorce, in any circumstance, rips a

---

[62] Jayna Solinger. "The Negative Effects of Divorce on Children" Quoting *Harper Book of American Quotations* (New York: Harper and Row, 1988), 192.

child apart, tossing him/her from one house to another, limiting time spent with his/her parents, and confusing him/her. There are very few reasons that would prove to be more beneficial for the parent to leave than to stay and endure his/her marriage. Usually it is more advantageous to children if their parents work through their differences rather than get a divorce.[63]

By any definition, divorce is a horrible word. There is no way to make the word sound better or make its effects less painful. According to the Webster's Dictionary, divorce is "the legal dissolution of marriage or the termination of an existing relationship or union." This definition makes the word seem formal and does not accurately display the feeling that sweeps over a person when the word is mentioned. A better definition of the depth of the word comes from a child named Whitney from an online interview, "Through the Eyes of a Child." Whitney says, "Divorce is like a thousand knives being thrown at one's heart or a slow, painful ride through Horror Mountain."[64] Her definition more accurately describes the feelings and emotions that go along with the mention of divorce. Most children would agree with this child's summary of divorce. To them, divorce is much more than a legal dissolution; it is their whole world being torn apart and thrown on the ground in pieces.

BY GOD'S GRACE LOVE GOD AND YOUR WIFE (2:16b)

If divorce is so horrific and cruel today, it was even more so in Malachi's day. Women had no rights and were often treated as not much more than property. So the prophet warns the husbands that they need to guard their hearts in regard to the marriage God gave them.

Malachi 2:16b | So guard yourselves in your spirit, and do not be faithless.

Twice in this passage Malachi urges his people to "take heed" to their spirits so that they would not 'deal treacherously' or be cruel through divorcing their wives (2:15-16).

---

http://www.public.iastate.edu/~rhetoric/105H16/cova/jlscova.html. Accessed 7 Aug 2017.

[63] Solinger, *Negative Effects*, ibid.

[64] "Whitney." *Through the Eyes of a Child* (Birmingham, MI: Divorce Online, 20 November 1998). http://web.archive.org/web/19981212024418/http://www.divorceonline.com, Accessed 7 Aug 2017.

Guard Your Heart

In these words, the prophet registers his conviction that the problem of unfaithfulness is rooted in man's spirit or heart. This is a much-needed corrective. We live in an age when people seek to excuse their unfaithfulness on the basis of their circumstances. But Malachi will have none of this. Unfaithfulness in every area of life flows from a heart that is not right with God. For this reason, the author of Proverbs urges: "Keep your heart with all diligence, For out of it spring the issues of life" (Prov 4:23). We must never let our heart lead us, for "the heart is deceitful above all things, and desperately sick; who can understand it?" (Jer 17:9). Instead of instructing yourself with your fallen heart, in order to preserve your marriage, you must instruct yourself with the Word of God in various teachings of the Word. For instance:

1. God is sovereign and gave me my spouse (Mt 19:6).
2. The point of marriage is not happiness but holiness, to learn how to love sacrificially and unconditionally as God loves me by putting off anger and putting on tenderness, kindness, and forgiveness (1 Pet 3:1-12; Eph 5:22-33).
3. Marriage is a picture of Christ's love for a church of forgiven sinners (Eph 5:22-33).
4. The only perfect spouse is God (Isaiah 54:5, "For your Maker is your husband, the LORD of hosts is his name; and the Holy One of Israel is your Redeemer, the God of the whole earth he is called.")
5. As believers, the only thing that can legitimately dissolve marriage is death (Rom 7:1-3), the breaking of the marriage covenant through adultery or other deviant sexual sin (Mt 19:6) or desertion by an unbeliever either by abandonment or abuse (1 Cor 7:15).

Tell the Ultimate Love Story with Your Marriage

Ultimate happiness comes from giving your life away, not to each other, though that is important. Ultimately happiness comes by each one of us giving ourselves to God. God created marriage as a picture to tell the story of His love for His Bride. Marriage is an expression of God's love for people who don't deserve it. The covenant of marriage tells more about our relationship with Christ than any mere human love story. "This mystery [of marriage] is profound, and I am saying that it refers to Christ and the church. So, let each one of you [as a husband] love his wife as himself, and let the wife see that she respects her husband" (Eph 5:32). Everything about marriage is meant to tell the greatest love story ever told. It is the story of how God can love the most unworthy people.

Conclusion

Marital love, though it is strong, is also imperfect. The Christian husband is to love his wife in a profound way. He is to love his bride as Christ loved his church and gave himself for her. The husband is called to provide for her and cherish her. There are many times when we fall short. We are not perfect. We need to remember to have patience with each other, because God is not finished with us yet. Our love for one another in marriage, though imperfect, should be unconditional.

In the same way, God's love is unconditional. The Bible says: "by grace you have been saved through faith. And this is not your own doing; it is the gift of God, not a result of works, so that no one may boast" (Eph 2:8-9). God's love is a free gift that He gives you when you surrender your whole life to His Son Jesus Christ. "He saved us, not because of works done by us in righteousness, but according to his own mercy, by the washing of regeneration and renewal of the Holy Spirit" (Titus 3:5).

5 | MALACHI 2:17-3:6
IF YOU LOVE ME, TRUST MY TIMING

For I the Lord do not change; therefore you, O children
of Jacob, are not consumed.
M ALACHI 3:6

I can't tell you who is going to be elected mayor, governor or president in the next political cycle. I don't know what gas prices or housing prices will be tomorrow. I don't know what college my children are going to choose. I don't know what tomorrow holds. But I know someone who does. We are going to meet him in this ancient message that Malachi preached. We need to trust the Lord. We need to wait on his perfect timing. It's hard to wait on God, but every moment of waiting is designed to increase our joy and trust in God.

Disillusionment had followed the rebuilding of the temple in the Prophet Malachi's day because, though decade followed decade, no supernatural event marked the return of the Lord to Zion. So far as could be judged the Jews had done their part, but God failed to fulfil his promises like the one found in Zechariah 8.

> Thus says the Lord: I have returned to Zion and will dwell in the midst of Jerusalem, and Jerusalem shall be called the faithful city, and the mountain of the Lord of hosts, the holy mountain. Thus says the Lord of hosts: Old men and old women shall again sit in the streets of Jerusalem, each with staff in hand because of great age. And the streets of

the city shall be full of boys and girls playing in its streets. — Zechariah 8:3-5

God's people felt the Almighty had forgotten his promises. His timing seemed completely off. They constantly complained to the Lord and accused him of many things, especially that he was favoring the wicked and forgetting the righteous. God seemed so silent. We often find ourselves feeling distant from God. What should the believer do? Just what God commanded those the believers in Malachi's day: trust the Lord.

TRUST GOD'S SILENCE (2:17)

Malachi 2:17 | You have wearied the Lord with your words. But you say, 'How have we wearied him?' By saying, 'Everyone who does evil is good in the sight of the Lord, and he delights in them.' Or by asking, 'Where is the God of justice?'

The Lord's delays were being taken and viewed as his absence. In turn the people live with a kind of practical atheism. Their question "Where is the God of justice?" was tantamount to doubting his existence. They no longer felt his presence or saw his blessing.

God's had a certain silence in the Old Testament. He was revealing things about the coming Messiah but not everything. In fact all the prophecies of the Old Testament about Christ are not only for the believers of the old covenant, but perhaps more so the new covenant. All of God's promises are for you as a believer in Christ. "Concerning this salvation, the prophets who prophesied about the grace that was to be yours searched and inquired carefully, inquiring what person or time the Spirit of Christ in them was indicating when he predicted the sufferings of Christ and the subsequent glories. It was revealed to them that they were serving not themselves but you, in the things that have now been announced to you through those who preached the good news to you by the Holy Spirit sent from heaven, things into which angels long to look" (1 Pet 1:10-12). God seems silent sometimes because he is doing something greater in us. He is conforming us to the image of Christ. There is always a reason for God's timing. God is always doing something good on our behalf (Rom 8:28). And yet it's true. We believe theologically that God is present with us. But practically we sometimes struggle with believing God is there. He seems at times to be distant.

Why is God Silent?

Just because God is not on your timetable, doesn't mean he's not listening. God often delays in answering our prayers.[65] Why does God delay in answering our prayers? What we will find is that God's silence is often due to our own falling short of his glory in various ways.

1. Our focus is off. At times the Lord sees that our attention is misdirected, and we ask with earthly instead of God-honoring motives. Our relationship with him should have priority over any earthly matter. Minds and prayers can become so fixed upon a need that our gaze shifts away from him. The Father may delay his answer until we refocus on him. "And you shall love the Lord your God with all your heart and with all your soul and with all your mind and with all your strength" (Mk 12:30). "But seek first the kingdom of God and his righteousness, and all these things will be added to you" (Mt 6:33).

2. God's plans are bigger than our plans. In other situations, God waits because the timing is not right for granting our request. Perhaps certain events must happen first, or people's thinking needs to be changed. "For my thoughts are not your thoughts, neither are your ways my ways, declares the Lord. For as the heavens are higher than the earth, so are my ways higher than your ways and my thoughts than your thoughts" (Isa 55:8-9).

3. God is growing us. There are also seasons when the Lord wants to stretch and grow our faith. One of the ways he accomplishes that is by having us watch for his response. The Holy Spirit will work in these times of waiting to mature us and bring forth righteous fruit (Gal 5:22-23).

4. Habitual sin characterizes our lives. We all fall short when it comes to God's standard of holiness, but some professing believers persist for a time in disobedience. A genuine believer is protected from living in disobedience as a lifestyle (1 Jn 5:18), but he may backslide for a time. Because of this the Lord may delay his answer so he can prompt us to confess our sin and turn back to him. "For the Lord disciplines the one he loves, and chastises every son whom he receives" (Heb 12:6). This chastisement may include a delay or a halt to answered prayer.

Waiting on the Lord isn't easy—faith and trust are needed (Heb 11:1). If his answer is delayed, check that 1) your focus is on him, 2) your

---

[65] The following section is adapted from Charles Stanley. *Waiting for Answers to Prayer* (Atlanta: InTouch Magazine, June 29, 2011).

trust is in his plans and not your own 3) you are submitted to his plan
to grow you, and 4) you aren't practicing habitual sin. Then believe that
his response will be for your good and his glory. I love Psalm 39:7, "And
now, O Lord, for what do I wait? My hope is in you."

Why Do the Evil Prosper?

The age-old problem raised by the apparent prosperity of the evil
man was an issue on everyone's mind in Malachi's day. It appeared that
God favored the wicked, and both Jeremiah (Jer 12:1) and Habakkuk
(Hab 1:2–4) had questioned God's just ordering of providence, while at
the same time maintaining their faith in God's ultimate righteousness.[66] It appeared to them that God favored evil men, seeing how the
evil people were prospering rather than being judged by God.[67] The
people of Israel in Malachi's day had hardened their hearts to the Lord.
They viewed their present circumstances as God being silent. To them,
it was like God was ignoring them.

When our hope is not in the Lord, our hearts become hard and
cynical like those in Jerusalem during Malachi's day. I read recently
about a man who had a large, bushy moustache. While he was sleeping,
some young pranksters smeared limburger cheese on his moustache.
When he awoke his first comment was, 'This room stinks!' He immediately went into another room and pronounced: 'This house stinks.' He
then stepped outside, and sniffed, and muttered, 'The whole world
stinks!' I've known some people who thought the whole world stank
when the real trouble was right beneath their own noses! Believers instead are called to "rejoice in the Lord always" (Phil 4:4).

Why Do We Get Angry with God?

Why do people get cynical and angry toward God? It is because
they construct some notion of what he must do and when he must do
it. If it does not happen according to their preconceived notion, they
conclude that he has failed. Malachi's people were upset with God because, in their opinion, he had not brought justice to the wicked on
their timetable. Anger toward God proceeds from a heart that is forgetful of his love, his perfect reputation and record, and his promises.

---

[66] Baldwin., 263.
[67] Cheung, *Malachi*, Kindle Locations 1285-1286.

This complaint was their way of expressing unhappiness with God for not sending the Messiah on their timetable. To their minds the Messiah was overdue. It was so clear to them, but it had not happened. Although God had demonstrated throughout their nation's history that he would be faithful to his promises, their faith in him was shaken. They took God's delay in fulfilling his promise to mean he was not going to keep his promise. So they felt abandoned by God while the wicked seemed to prosper.

How is God Wearied?

Malachi leaves no doubt about the seriousness of their cynicism. He says it had "wearied the Lord" (2:17). Most of us are not accustomed to the idea of God getting tired. We think of the words of the prophet Isaiah: "Have you not known? Have you not heard? The everlasting God, the Lord, the creator of the ends of the earth neither faints nor is weary" (Isa 40:28). Of course, we understand that God never gets truly "weary." He is omnipotent. The expression is an anthropopathism – attributing human emotional attributes to God in order to help us understand a divine concept in human terms. Malachi says that the people of Israel had "wearied the Lord" with their words. God is never said to be wearied with human prayers and questions but only with human sin.[68] The prophet Isaiah says it well, "You have not bought me sweet cane with money, or satisfied me with the fat of your sacrifices. But you have *burdened me with your sins*; you have wearied me with your iniquities" (Isa 43:24).

What then was it that wearied God? It was a sinful understanding of God where God is somehow absent, uninterested, and lacked justice. The priests were saying, "Everyone who does evil is good in the sight of the Lord, and he delights in them." And they were asking: "Where is the God of justice?" (2:17). The root of God's weariness was their unbelieving hearts and their cynical prayers. Remember it was the priests who first said that their worship was a burden and said, "What a weariness" (1:13). But here it is God who is offended by Israel's sins. It's like Isaiah 43:24 says, "You have burdened me with your sins; you have wearied me with your iniquities."

---

[68] Baldwin, 263-264.

Asaph: God is Not Silent

God will most certainly judge the wicked, but it will be in his time and his way. "For my thoughts are not your thoughts, neither are your ways my ways" (Isa 55:8). If we only look at the fabric of time, we as mere humans will be confused and despairing as God's people in Malachi's day and as Asaph in the Psalms. Asaph in Psalm 73 begins to have a cynical heart, but he brings it to the Lord. Listen to his heart cry and note his conclusion. "Truly God is good to Israel, to those who are pure in heart. But as for me, my feet had almost stumbled, my steps had nearly slipped. For I was envious of the arrogant when I saw the prosperity of the wicked" (vs. 1-3). "Behold, these are the wicked; always at ease, they increase in riches. All in vain have I kept my heart clean and washed my hands in innocence" (vs. 12). "But when I thought how to understand this, it seemed to me a wearisome task, until I went into the sanctuary of God; then I discerned their end. Truly you set them in slippery places; you make them fall to ruin. How they are destroyed in a moment, swept away utterly by terrors!" (vs. 16-19).

Asaph had to consider the ultimate and final judgment of God before he could understand how he might trust in God for God's final justice. Asaph's conclusion was that God is indeed not at all silent. He's simply on a different timetable than us. Why is God's timing so different from ours? Why is he so slow in bringing swift justice? The apostle Peter has the answer: "The Lord is not slow to fulfill his promise as some count slowness, but is patient toward you, not wishing that any should perish, but that all should reach repentance" (2 Pet 3:9). God is patient in bringing people to himself. But there will come a day when he comes in judgment upon the wicked and "the day of the Lord will come like a thief, and then the heavens will pass away with a roar" (2 Pet 3:10). Jesus is coming both as Savior and as Judge. You can be sure of that.

TRUST GOD'S SON (3:1-4)

The ultimate answer to evil is answered in the cross of Christ. Here we see the God patiently answering his people. They were complaining that God's promises were not fulfilled – as if God had forgotten to be faithful and true. The passage that follows is quite the surprise. Not only is Messiah coming, but he will "suddenly come to his temple" (3:1).

The Son's Messenger

Malachi 3:1 | Behold, I send my messenger, and he will prepare the way
   before me. And the Lord whom you seek will suddenly come to his
   temple; and the messenger of the covenant in whom you delight,
   behold, he is coming, says the Lord of hosts.

The Lord here assures his people that he has not forgotten his
promise to send the Messiah. The one whom they were seeking would
be preceded by a special messenger from God (John the Baptist). John
Benton writes: "John the Baptist was like a herald going before the
royal procession to indicate the route that the king would take and to
make preparations for his coming."[69] God's messenger John the Baptist
would precede Jesus like Elijah preceded Elisha. John is a messenger
– the mailman, if you would. He "will prepare the way" for Jesus. Fur-
thermore, the Messiah would "suddenly come to his temple" (3:1). The
Lord probably chose to emphasize this because of the people thought
the second temple was far inferior to first temple, built by Solomon.
Here the Lord tells them that this second temple would have a glory all
its own, a glory which could never be matched by Solomon's temple,
because this new temple would be visited by the Messiah himself! The
hearts of the people may very well have leaped within them as they
heard Malachi assure them that the Messiah would come to their temple. Yet they could not have been elated for long. The reason? Malachi
proceeded to deliver a stinging message. Yes, the Messiah was coming,
but he would not do what they were expecting. He would come to deal
with the sins of Israel!

The Son's Mission

Malachi 3:2 | But who can endure the day of his coming, and who can
   stand when he appears? For he is like a refiner's fire and like fullers'
   soap.

Malachi makes this point by saying that the Messiah would come
"like a refiner's fire" and "like fullers' soap" (3:2). His mission is to purify a people for his own glory. As the refiner removes impurities from
silver and the fuller (launderer) removes filth from clothes, so the Messiah would come to cleanse the people of Israel. This cleansing work

[69] Benton, 92.

would apply to all. Even the religious leaders ("the sons of Levi"—3:3) would not be exempt from it. The Messiah would purify them so they would give "an offering in righteousness" (3:3).[70] What an amazing prophecy of Christ's church who are all "a royal priesthood, a holy nation, a people for his own possession" (1 Pet 2:9). Jesus comes to cleanse and purify his people in the inner most part of their souls. He does this through conversion and regeneration.

The Son's Worship

Malachi 3:3-4 | He will sit as a refiner and purifier of silver, and he will purify the sons of Levi and refine them like gold and silver, and they will bring offerings in righteousness to the Lord. Then the offering of Judah and Jerusalem will be pleasing to the Lord as in the days of old and as in former years.

The refiner who sits and concentrates all his attention on the metal in the crucible depicts the Lord's concern for the holiness of his people. He begins at his sanctuary (cf. Eze 9:6) with the sons of Levi: to purify them until they present "offerings in righteousness" (3:3). Christ comes with the power of the Spirit to regenerate the hearts of his people, and they respond with worship. He transforms them into "living stones" which "are being built up as a spiritual house, to be a holy priesthood, to offer spiritual sacrifices acceptable to God through Jesus Christ" who is the chief Cornerstone (1 Pet 2:5-6). Only in the spiritual house that God is building will the offerings be infinitely superior and "pleasing to the Lord as in the days of old and as in former years" (3:4). What a delightful prophecy about you and me. Christ comes to us as a refiner and purifier. Oh, how he has refined our hearts by the conviction and regenerating work of the Holy Spirit.

Sadly, the second temple would be destroyed in 70AD when the Romans under General Titus, surrounded the city of Jerusalem, overran it, and tore down the temple leaving it in a heap of rubble. It is said that at the fall of Jerusalem, the last surviving Jews of the city fled to the temple, because it was the strongest and most secure building in the city. Roman soldiers surrounded it, and one drunken soldier started a fire that soon engulfed the whole building. Ornate gold detail work in the roof melted down in the cracks between the stone walls of

---

[70] Ellsworth., 66-67.

the temple, and to retrieve the gold, the Roman commander ordered that the temple be dismantled stone by stone. The destruction was so complete that today they have true difficulty learning exactly where the foundation of the temple was.[71] Let us be clear then that Malachi is not referring to a physical temple. He's not even talking about the physical "sons of Levi." Peter makes it clear that the church of Jesus (Gentiles grafted into the believing Jewish tree, cf Rom 11:17). All that to say Christ is the ultimate Cornerstone of the true temple, his church. All those who trust in him are "living stones," a part of the "spiritual house" that God is building (1 Pet 2:5-8). Christ builds his new temple of living stones and "the gates of hell shall not prevail against it" (Mt 16:18).

TRUST GOD'S SALVATION (3:5-6)

Malachi then warns of the judgment that is coming: those who do not draw near to God for salvation, God will draw near to them in judgment.

Malachi 3:5 | Then I will draw near to you for judgment. I will be a swift witness against the sorcerers, against the adulterers, against those who swear falsely, against those who oppress the hired worker in his wages, the widow and the fatherless, against those who thrust aside the sojourner, and do not fear me, says the Lord of hosts.

Salvation is by Grace

God could immediately judge people for their many sins (of which Malachi only lists a few). But instead, they are not consumed because of the Lord's desire for mercy and grace. God has always been a God of grace. Graham Scroggie said, "They that wait upon the Lord will also wait for him."[72] God is "patient toward you, not wishing that any should perish, but that all should reach repentance" (2 Pet 3:9). Malachi gives the promise of God's unchangeable nature.

Malachi 3:6 | I the Lord do not change; therefore you, O children of Jacob, are not consumed.

He is a God of mercy and grace – this is the reason God's people were not consumed for their sins. God describes himself to Moses in Exodus 34:6-7, "The LORD passed before him and proclaimed, The

---

[71] Ray Steadman. *What's This World Coming to: An Expository Study of Matthew 24-25, the Olivet Discourse* (Ventura, CA: Regal Books, 1986).
[72] Graham Scroggie. *Soul-Depths and Soul-Heights*, 1874.

LORD, the LORD, a God merciful and gracious, slow to anger, and abounding in steadfast love and faithfulness, keeping steadfast love for thousands, forgiving iniquity and transgression and sin, but who will by no means clear the guilty, visiting the iniquity of the fathers on the children and the children's children, to the third and the fourth generation." From beginning to end, God's nature is merciful and gracious, slow to anger, and abounding in *hesed* – unrelenting love. This love pursues us all the way to the cross of Jesus Christ. The cross is a declaration of forgiveness for those who fear God enough to believe, and it is a declaration of guilt for those who do not fear God and do not believe. God has a long wick, but because God is *just*, he does get angry. Those who neglect or reject God's mercy will receive his just punishment. God desires to show mercy, but if someone rejects or neglects his mercy, because he is good and just, he will never acquit the guilty.

Salvation is Necessary because God is Angry

The profound reality of God's coming judgment is in Malachi 3:5, "Then I will draw near to you for judgment." The *"then"* of verse 5 has not yet come—the day of Judgment—but it will come when Jesus returns. For his people, Jesus is a witness for the defense. For those who are not his people, Jesus is a witness for the prosecution. And by the time Jesus arrives in his second coming, the trial is over, and the judgment is swift. This can easily lead us to stand afar from the world with pride, instead of dwelling in it with love. We will be tempted to act as judge since it seems like God is taking so long. Remember you and I are not the Judge. That job is already taken.

Sinful Anger

Anger is often sinful for human beings, but it is never wrong for God to be angry. Anger is a reality in the human heart, and it is something we must control, or it will control us. The Bible tells us to "be angry and sin not" (Eph 4:26). Most often anger is condemned in the Bible because among mankind it is motivated mostly by sinful desires. Charles Haddon Spurgeon clearly taught that God will root out sinful anger out of his people. Consider his words: "Do not say, 'I cannot help having a bad temper.' Friend, you must help it. Pray to God to help you overcome it at once, for either you must kill it, or it will kill you. You cannot carry a bad temper into heaven." Anger is often one of the top problems in marriage. It is often seen either in the withdrawal of a spouse in the marriage or else in explosive indignation. Both are symptoms of a larger underlying root: sinful anger. Yet anger is not always sinful. Anger is an emotion God has given to all humanity as a tool to maintain a passion for holiness and righteousness. We all have anger in our lives. It is something that exists because things are not right in the universe. Anger defined simply, is taking an emotional stand for one's convictions of right and wrong. It is saying, "I'm against something." Anger comes when we recognize things are not right in the world. That kind of anger can be very good or it can be very bad, depending on your focus. If anger is self-focused, then it is sinful anger. If we are angry because God's glory has been offended it can be righteous indignation.

Sovereign Anger

God is angry. As Christians, we need to realize that anger is not in and of itself sinful. Anger is a holy and perfect attribute of God—it is part of His justice. Psalm 7:11, "God judges the righteous, and God is angry with the wicked every day." God is angry against one thing: sin. Any time man ventures outside of God's control and sovereign lordship, we call that sin. 1 John 3:4, "sin is the transgression of the law." When we venture outside of God's rule over us, we have betrayed God's lordship and usurped his throne. When sin occurs in the universe, God meticulously demands justices. The fury of his holiness and goodness boils against sin.

The Bible says that on this day Jesus Christ will come "in flaming fire taking vengeance on them that know not God, and that obey not the gospel of our Lord Jesus Christ" (2 Thess 1:8). The mouths that right now are blaspheming God will be eternally stopped on the day that Christ returns. Every knee will bow and every tongue will confess that Jesus Christ is Lord. After Christ's coming, we will all face him. He will be sitting on an awesome radiant throne of judgment, and it says he is the one "from whose face the earth and the heaven fled away" (Rev 20:11). The reality of God's anger with the world should not lead us to pride, but to humility, because in the judgment of the world, we see the judgment we deserve. Knowing that God is angry and that there is a coming judgment of the world helps me to know that God's silence is not *indifference*—it should lead me to faith. Knowing that God is angry and there is a coming judgment of the world helps me to know that what feels like judgment now is refinement—it should lead me to *grow* and worship, even in pain. Knowing that God is angry and that there is a coming judgment of the world helps me to restrain my own indifference—it should lead me to *mission*.

Salvation is Available from a Changeless God

Malachi closes this section with the good news of the Gospel.

Malachi 3:6 | For I the Lord do not change; therefore you, O children of Jacob, are not consumed.

God answers Israel's accusations by telling them of Jesus' soon arrival. He is coming to prove they were wrong, in person. God does reveal himself in human history, breaking the silence in the Second Person of his divine Son. "But when the fullness of time had come, God sent forth his Son, born of woman, born under the law, to redeem those who were under the law, so that we might receive adoption as sons" (Gal 4:4-5). Jesus is the ultimate revelation of God (Heb 1:1-2). "Christ is the visible image of the invisible God. He existed before anything was created and is supreme over all creation" (Col 1:15, NLT). Yet Jesus is not the last word God will speak. Jesus will be "revealed from heaven with his mighty angels" at his second coming (1 Thess 1:7). Jesus' crucifixion proves that the evil of this world is never out of God's judicial watch. Don't mistake his silence for approval or his slowness for indifference. He sees. He knows. He cares. For the Christian, he paid the ultimate price to make it right, and one day he will make all things new (Isa 43:18; Rev 21:5). For the non-Christian, know that Judgement Day will come suddenly—today is your day to turn from your sin and trust in Jesus. Believe and experience God as loving Father, for if you don't, you will experience him as a wrathful judge. He will witness for his children, and he will surely witness against his enemies (Psa 1:4-6; Psa 2; cf. Mal 3:5-6).

Conclusion

You may not think God is angry right now, but he is. It is his divine patience and mercy that has held back the Judgement Day. God is patiently waiting for one final day when he will bring justice to every injustice, and he will thrust in his harvesting sickle into the earth, and gather all men to him (Mt 9:37-38). For now, in mercy, patience and grace, he is gathering his children in. Consider again St. Peter's word recorded in 2 Peter 3:3-13, "Knowing this first of all, that scoffers will come in the last days with scoffing, following their own sinful desires. They will say, 'Where is the promise of his coming? For ever since the fathers fell asleep, all things are continuing as they were from the beginning of creation.' For they deliberately overlook this fact, that the heavens existed long ago, and the earth was formed out of water and through water by the word of God, and that by means of these the world that then existed was deluged with water and perished. But by the same word the heavens and earth that now exist are stored up for fire, being kept until the day of judgment and destruction of the ungodly. But do not overlook this one fact, beloved, that with the Lord one day is as a thousand years, and a thousand years as one day. The Lord is not slow to fulfill his promise as some count slowness, but is patient toward you, not wishing that any should perish, but that all should reach repentance. But the day of the Lord will come like a thief, and then the heavens will pass away with a roar, and the heavenly bodies will be burned up and dissolved, and the earth and the works that are done on it will be exposed. Since all these things are thus to be dissolved, what sort of people ought you to be in lives of holiness and godliness, waiting for and hastening the coming of the day of God, because of which the heavens will be set on fire and dissolved, and the heavenly bodies will melt as they burn! But according to his promise we are waiting for new heavens and a new earth in which righteousness dwells."

May the Lord help us to trust in his mercy, and pray for the salvation of many of our loved ones, friends, and even our enemies. Let us trust God's timing. "Wait for the Lord; be strong, and let your heart take courage; wait for the Lord!" (Psa 27:14).

6 | MALACHI 3:7-15

IF YOU LOVE ME RECEIVE MY BLESSING

Will man rob God? Yet you are robbing me. But you say,
'How have we robbed you?' In your tithes and contributions.
MALACHI 3:8

God's nature is first loving and generous and kind. He is just, of course, but he takes no pleasure "in the death of the wicked" but wishes the wicked would "turn and live" and receive the blessing of the Lord (Eze 18:23). He delights to forgive us and promises to give genuine believers "every spiritual blessing" in Christ (Eph 1:3). God has a prerequisite for blessing us. He wants total surrender. Listen to C.S. Lewis, author of the Chronicles of Narnia, in his last sermon he ever preached on January 29, 1956. "God claims all, because He is love and must bless. He cannot bless us unless he has us. When we try to keep within us an area that is our own, we try to keep an area of death. Therefore, in love, he claims all. There's no bargaining with him."[73]

Our God is a God who loves to bless his people. Even though the people in Malachi's day were blind to his love and generosity, God promises to infinitely bless these very undeserving people. We are probably more undeserving today than the people of Malachi's day.

---

[73] C.S. Lewis, "A Slip of the Tongue," in *The Weight of Glory and Other Addresses* (New York: Simon & Schuster, Touchstone, 1996), 137ff. *This was Lewis' last sermon and was delivered January 29, 1956.*

They didn't know as much as we do – they were waiting for Messiah – we live after his coming. How blessed we are. Do you know how blessed you are at this moment? The people of Malachi's day were blind to it. They were blind to his tender mercies.

The reason we are so often caught in the traps of sin is because we have forgotten that we are citizens of another city. Yes, we are living in this world, but we need to be living for another world altogether. If you are born again, you are united with Christ; you are seated with Him in the heavenly places; and you are therefore "blessed with all spiritual blessings" in Christ (Eph 1:3). We need to live with this constant focus. We need to live for another world entirely. Oh, how God wants to bless his people. This is Malachi's message.

GOD'S BLESSING OF RELENTLESS PURSUIT (3:6)

Malachi 3:6 | For I the Lord do not change; therefore you, O children of Jacob, are not consumed.

Change is a fact of life for every person on earth. We grow either better or worse, but we never stay the same. God is perfect. He cannot grow better or worse. He is the standard of all that is good. Because God's goodness is unchangeable, we don't have to worry about God changing his mind about his love for us.

If he has fixed his love upon, then it has always been this way. He has loved you with an everlasting love (Jer 31:3). That's why we are not consumed. Certainly, God is speaking at least of physical consummation, i.e. death and extermination. The Jewish race would have been devoured by her neighbors if it wasn't for the sovereign intervention of God. Everyone from Pharaoh to Sennacherib to Nebuchadnezzar could have wiped Israel off the map, were it not for God – were it not for grace. And were it not for grace the entire human race would be consumed physically and spiritually. He could have allowed our hearts to harden. But God has always graciously sent us prophets. Today we have God's completed, sufficient Word. He gives us teachers and preachers of clay. Despite their many imperfections, he uses them, even in spite of them. All grace. All God's glorious grace. That's why we are not consumed. We deserve to die physically. We deserve to perish spiritually in hell. Yet God is not willing that you should perish. His Son perished in your place.

Aren't you glad that our gracious God never changes? He never wavers in his love for you. There will never be a day when you sin, and God says: "I change my mind. How did I ever set my love upon you? I give up on you." That will never happen. Why? God's faithful, covenant love never changes. He chose you "to the praise of his glorious grace" (Eph 1:7). He will "never leave you nor forsake you" (Heb 13:5).

GOD'S BLESSING OF RETURNING TO US (3:7)

Malachi 3:7 | From the days of your fathers you have turned aside from my statutes and have not kept them. Return to me, and I will return to you, says the Lord of hosts. But you say, 'How shall we return?'

Though God's people had been rebellious for generations, God is still there bidding them to return to him. This is God's nature. He is good and gracious. His love is unrelenting. His grace truly is greater than all our sins. God is calling his people to return to him with a life of repentance.

Our record is clear. Like the people in Malachi's day, we have turned aside from God's statutes in many ways. There is a part of us that will "suppress the truth in unrighteousness" (Rom 1:18). We lie to ourselves that we are not that bad. But we are worse than we imagine. We cannot even judge ourselves rightly because our hearts are twisted by sin (Jer 17:9). We are commanded not to "lean to our own understanding" (Prov 3:5) when it comes to our heart. Don't trust your heart. Trust God instead.

Malachi 3:7a | From the days of your fathers you have turned aside from my statutes and have not kept them.

Malachi says, this is nothing new. This has been going on for generations. Malachi is far from idealizing past generations. A hundred years earlier Ezra and Zechariah said the same thing (*cf* Ezra 9:7; Zech 1:2).[74]

The Promise: I Will Return to You

But God gives us a sweet invitation – an invitation to return!

Malachi 3:7b | Return to me, and I will return to you, says the Lord of hosts.

---

[74] Baldwin, 268.

No matter where you've strayed, God will return to you. You simply need to take the step of repentance toward him. Our God is a pardoning God! James 4:8-10 calls us as New Covenant saints to return in the same way: "Draw near to God, and he will draw near to you. Cleanse your hands, you sinners, and purify your hearts, you double-minded. Be wretched and mourn and weep. Let your laughter be turned to mourning and your joy to gloom. Humble yourselves before the Lord, and he will exalt you." The term "draw near" in James 4:8 originally referred to the priests who were to "draw near" and offer sacrifices on the Day of Atonement. This points not only to forgiveness of sin, but to full reconciliation. God has released us from his wrath. Now we can return to him in shalom – well-being. Now God has opened the way for you to be restored—he's granted you access through Jesus' blood. He invites you to draw close to him. These are words of *fellowship* and *communion*.

Remember what David said in Psalm 24? You and I would do well to come to God like this every day. "Who shall ascend into the hill of the LORD? or who shall stand in his holy place? He that hath clean hands, and a pure heart; who hath not lifted up his soul unto vanity, nor sworn deceitfully. He shall receive the blessing from the LORD" (Psa 24:3-5). Ladies, you don't go to your wedding day with dirty fingernails. And you don't go to the Lord with dirty sin in your heart and in your life. The heart touched by God hungers for righteousness and for clean hands. The true believer cannot live comfortably in sin. The Spirit within us brings conviction so great so that we have a heart for holiness.

The Prerequisite: Return to Me

What is God inviting us to do? "Return to me" (3:7b) is an invitation to repent. He calls us to forsake all others and be joined to Him. We know what this means. Men, when you saw your wife for the first time, nobody had to tell you to draw near to her. There's an abandonment in this word. We are called to forsake anything that has come between our soul and the Savior. Drawing near to God means my heart's desire is for intimacy with the living God.

The Israelites now ask, "But you say, 'How shall we return?'" (3:7c). That's a good question. The answer from God is: Give up your greed and materialism and I will show you my generosity. Sadly, it seems the people were not asking sincerely. They were saying, "What more can we do to return to you? We are in a right standing before you." They were not right, but only self-righteous. In spite of the hypocrisy and self-righteousness that we suffer from, God is a God of blessing. God gives the people a simple test: tithe to me and I will open the windows of heaven to you.

GOD'S BLESSING OF HEAVEN RENDING (3:8-11)

The people ask, "How shall we return?" Show us how to repent. Malachi answers in the same way Jesus did. Where ever your money is, that's what you love. Your checkbook tells us where your heart is. Jesus says, "For where your treasure is, there your heart will be also" (Mt 6:21).

Stop Robbing Me

Malachi charges the people with robbing God.

Malachi 3:8 | Will man rob God? Yet you are robbing me. But you say, 'How have we robbed you?' In your tithes and contributions.

Malachi brings forth his case by giving us an example from the life of Jacob. Malachi may have cited the example of Jacob to highlight the people's sin. Jacob went to Paddan Aram to seek a wife. He was there 14 years before he married Rachel (Gen 28:28) and 20 years in total serving "Uncle Laban." It was a kind of "exile" for Jacob. After Jacob's exile in Paddan Aram, when he 'returned' both to the promised land and to the Lord, he built an altar at Bethel, and he offered a tithe to the Lord according to his vow there. Consider Jacob's promise in Genesis 28:20-22 (*cf* also Gen 35:1-7). "Then Jacob made a vow, saying, "If God will be with me and will keep me in this way that I go, and will give me bread to eat and clothing to wear, so that I come again to my father's house in peace, then the Lord shall be my God, and this stone, which I have set up for a pillar, shall be God's house. And of all that you give me I will give a full tenth to you." He seems to fulfill the vow in Genesis 35.

When Jacob's descendants in Malachi's time similarly returned from their exile, they rebuilt the altar at Jerusalem, but they were grossly negligent in offering their tithes (*cf* Neh 13:10-13). Nehemiah had rebuked them and "then all Judah brought the tithe of the grain, wine, and oil into the storehouses" (Neh 13:12). This negligence may have seemed justified because of crop failure, drought and pestilence

(3:10–11) which would have been more than enough to deter such complacent worshippers. The Lord reveals, however, that these natural disasters were the result, and not the cause, of the nation's disobedience (3:8; *cf* Hag 1:6, 9–11; 2:16–19).[75]

Can Christians Be Cursed?

God says to the whole nation:

Malachi 3:9 | You are cursed with a curse, for you are robbing me, the whole nation of you.

For Israel, "the curse probably took the form of drought, poor crops and economic depression. Yet even while the curse was in progress... the people were continuing to rob God."[76] For the Christian, our curse has been removed in Christ. "Christ redeemed us from the curse of the law by becoming a curse for us—for it is written, 'Cursed is everyone who is hanged on a tree'" (Gal 3:13). Not only is there no longer a curse for us, he has put within our hearts the Holy Spirit so that Christians are prone to generosity. He says he causes us to "walk in his statutes and to keep his judgments" (Eze 36:26-27). Yet there is a pattern of consequences for the Christian who does not honor God with their finances. We do reap what we sow (Gal 6:7). Though we are never condemned because of Christ (Rom 8:1), it is possible for the Christian to suffer the consequences of robbing God. I've heard people say "Why should I give God any of my money." As Christians we can never ask that question, because the premise is false. It's not my money. What we ask as stewards and managers of God is: "How much of God's money should I keep?" "The earth is the LORD's and the fullness thereof, the world and those who dwell therein" (Psa 24:1).

It would be nice on our paycheck where it had your name if it would be written in bold letters: "this check belongs to the Lord Jesus Christ". You are named as the manager. Or how about that Debit card or bank account. All your accounts are in the Lord's name, and you are an authorized manager. Every time you go to spend money you ought to have the mentality that it is the Lord's money, and you say, "Ok, Lord, I'm going to spend some of your money right now." The Bible says a lot about how to handle money in a godly way. Jesus in his own

---

[75] Hugenberger. *Malachi*, 888.
[76] J. E. Smith, J. E. *The Minor Prophets* (Joplin, MO: College Press, 1994) Mal 3:9.

teaching talks about finances 25% of the time. Remember that the Bible nowhere teaches that money itself is evil. It is not money or possessions that are at fault; it is the men who use them. Scripture talks about wealth and money over 800 different times. Whether Old or New Testament, we are commanded in Proverbs how to be wise with our money. We are to give God the firstfruits – the first portion of our income. "Honor the LORD with your wealth and with the firstfruits of all your produce; then your barns will be filled with plenty, and your vats will be bursting with wine" (Pro 3:9–10). Moses gave the same command in the law given at Sinai. "The best of the firstfruits of your ground you shall bring into the house of the LORD your God" (Exo 23:19). We are called to seek God and his kingdom first (Mt 6:33). We must never forget God's promise of provision for all his children, "And my God will supply every need of yours according to his riches in glory in Christ Jesus" (Phil 4:19).

What Was the Old Testament Tithe?

Malachi commands the people:

Malachi 3:10 | Bring the full tithe into the storehouse, that there may be food in my house.

John MacArthur explains what the full Old Testament tithe was.

> Two kinds of giving are taught consistently throughout Scripture: giving to the government (always compulsory), and giving to God (always voluntary). The issue has been greatly confused, however, by some who misunderstand the nature of the Old Testament tithes. Tithes were not primarily gifts to God, but taxes for funding the national budget in Israel. Because Israel was a theocracy, the Levitical priests acted as the civil government. So the Levite's tithe (Lev 27:30-33) was a precursor to today's income tax, as was a second annual tithe required by God to fund a national festival (Deut 14:22-29). Smaller taxes were also imposed on the people by the law (Lev 19:9-10; Exo 23:10-11). So the total giving required of the Israelites was not 10 percent, but well over 20 percent. All that money was used to operate the nation. New Testament believers are never commanded to tithe. Matthew 22:15-22 and Romans 13:1-7 tell us about the only required giving in the church age, which is the paying of taxes

to the government. Interestingly enough, we in America presently pay between 20 and 30 percent of our income to the government – a figure very similar to the requirement under the theocracy of Israel. The guideline for our giving to God and his work is found in 2 Corinthians 9:6-7: 'Now this I say, he who sows sparingly shall also reap sparingly; and he who sows bountifully shall also reap bountifully. Let each one do just as he has purposed in his heart; not grudgingly or under compulsion; for God loves a cheerful giver.[77]

How Should the New Testament Saint Give?

The standard for the law of faith or the law of the Spirit is higher than Moses' law. If they saw the truth in a dark, fuzzy mirror, we who see clearly should be known not by mere law keeping, but true generosity that goes beyond the Old Testament standard. We should be personally involved in the finances of the local church as well as missions, and many other areas of benevolence outside the church. We ought to give not only of our time but also our treasure.

People have asked me: Should I tithe to God? My answer is yes! But be careful not to let your generosity be hinged to an Old Testament concept. A tithe is a good place for a New Covenant believer to start, but we should not be content there. We should be known as those who give to the storehouse of God's people cheerfully and not under obligation. "The end of this matter is that not merely our money or time, but our whole selves—body, soul, and spirit—are God's, and therefore we are to honor God wholly with all we are." [78]

Paul wrote, "You are not your own; you were bought at a price. Therefore honor God with your body" (1 Cor 6:19–20). He said, "Therefore, I urge you, brothers, in view of God's mercy, to offer your bodies as living sacrifices, holy and pleasing to God—this is your spiritual act of worship" (Rom 12:1). If you follow the resources in your life, they will tell you where your heart is. One of the ways we show love is through generosity and provision and care. As we said already, Jesus says, "For where your treasure is, there your heart will be also" (Mt 6:21). Money is the chief indicator of where your priorities are. We as believers are

---

[77] John MacArthur. *Does God require me to give a tithe of all I earn?* (Sun Valley, CA: Grace to You, August 18, 2016), https://www.gty.org/library/questions/QA144. Accessed 22 Feb 2017.

[78] Boice. *Minor Prophets*, 604.

all stewards. The biblical teaching of stewardship is that I'm a manager of things I do not own. Ultimately things don't belong to me; ultimately everything belongs to God. God has given me possessions, income, a home, a place to sleep. And He's given those things to us that we might manage them in such a way that it glorifies God.

Open the Floodgates of Heaven

Malachi 3:10b | "… put me to the test, says the Lord of hosts, if I will not open the windows of heaven for you and pour down for you a blessing until there is no more need.

God is a good God. The Israelites ask, "How shall we return?" God answers: "Bring the full tithe into the storehouse [the Temple treasury]" (3:10a). Today we are to give to the ministries of the local church so that Christ might build his church, "and the gates of hell will not prevail against it" (Mt 16:18). God says put me to the test! God's blessing comes by the believer obeying God. All spiritual relationships with God start with obedience. What are the blessings God is talking about?

1. Certainly, the blessing begins with God's presence.

Oh that you would rend the heavens and come down, that the mountains might quake at your presence. —Isaiah 64:1

God is preparing a place for you (Jn 14:1-3), and he is preparing you for that inheritance. God blesses his people. Yes, the Bible says we will inherit a city that has gold for streets, a river of life, a tree of life, a city that never sleeps but always praises God, a place of music and delightful learning and conversation (Psa 16:11), but most of all, our inheritance is the triune God. We will bask in his fellowship forever. He says, "You will be my people and I will be your God" (Rev 21:3). He says, I will "wipe away every tear from your eyes, and death shall be no more, neither shall there be mourning, nor crying, nor pain anymore, for the former things have passed away" (Rev 21:4). This is the ultimate blessing that God gives in Malachi and throughout his word to us.

2. The blessing of God's provision.

Malachi 3:10 | I will… pour down for you a blessing until there is no more need.

"And my God will supply every need of yours according to his riches in glory in Christ Jesus. To our God and Father be glory forever and ever. Amen" (Phil 4:19-20). We serve the God who gave Elijah food from a raven in the wilderness. He's the God that can rain manna from heaven. He's the God who can always make something out of nothing. God can do it all—with or without you. God is going to provide, and he can do it any way he wants to. If we will walk with him by faith, he will pour down his blessings "until there is no more need." What provision!

3. The blessing of God's protection & prosperity.

Malachi 3:11 | I will rebuke the devourer for you, so that it will not destroy the fruits of your soil, and your vine in the field shall not fail to bear, says the Lord of hosts.

For the Old Testament believer, this meant God would prosper Israel as a nation. That has all now been fulfilled in Christ. These land promises are now fulfilled in Jesus and his church. "Every spiritual blessing" is ours in Christ (Eph 1:3). "The promise to Abraham and his offspring" was "that he would be heir of the world" (Rom 4:13). It doesn't get bigger than that. My ultimate blessing will be in the world to come where I am an "heir of God and a joint heir with Christ" (Rom 8:17). The imagery of "inheritance" in the New Testament (Mt 5:5; Heb 11:8-10; 1 Pet 1:4-5) derives from the Old Testament terminology associated with Israel's inheritance of the land (Exo 32:13; Lev 20:24; Num 26:3–56; Deut 3:28). In other words, Israel's inheritance of the land of Canaan is a foretaste of the Christian's inheritance in the regeneration of all things on the New Earth. Remember Exodus 32:13 where Moses says to the children of Israel: "Remember Abraham, Isaac, and Israel, your servants, to whom you swore by your own self, and said to them, 'I will multiply your offspring as the stars of heaven, and all this land that I have promised I will give to your offspring, and they shall inherit it forever.'" This is a direct reference to the Abrahamic covenant. God's not only going to save Abraham and all who believe. He's going to give them the promised land without any threat of devastation from crop failure or drought ("I will rebuke the devourer") which is ultimately fulfilled in the New Earth.

Rebuke the Devourer on Earth

What does it mean when God says:

Malachi 3:11 | I will rebuke the devourer for you, so that it will not destroy the fruits of your soil, and your vine in the field shall not fail to bear, says the Lord of hosts.

For Israel in Malachi's day, it meant God would protect them from pests and droughts that would kill their crops. For the Christian today, the promises are both earthly and eternal. God promises to care for our needs (Phil 4:19). It could sometimes mean that if you lack in generosity as a Christian, the Lord may at times allow you to suffer loss in your life. A dear accountant friend used to say to me, "I can live far better on 90% than on 100%." While the tithe is never mandated for the New Testament believer, if possible, it is a great place to start.

Behold Our Generous God

The whole point of the matter is that God is a generous God. For those who are generous and selfless, yet wise, he will give more to manage. God says:

Malachi 3:10 | Put me to the test, says the Lord of hosts, if I will not open the windows of heaven for you and pour down for you a blessing until there is no more need.

God is a God of abundance and kindness. He lacks nothing. He seeks generous saints who will be good stewards of sharing his wealth. Consider New Testament words on wealth: "As for the rich in this present age, charge them not to be haughty, nor to set their hopes on the uncertainty of riches, but on God, who richly provides us with everything to enjoy. They are to do good, to be rich in good works, to be generous and ready to share, thus storing up treasure for themselves as a good foundation for the future, so that they may take hold of that which is truly life" (1 Tim 6:17-19). The rich were made rich so they would as believers "be generous and ready to share." Our God wants to open up the floodgates of heaven. His nature and desire is to bless you so you can bless others.

GOD'S BLESSING OF TESTIMONY RAISING (3:12)

Malachi 3:12 | Then all nations will call you blessed, for you will be a land of delight, says the Lord of hosts.

One of the greatest blessings is one of influence. God's people were ruining their testimony before the other nations. "Israel's neighbors knew that she was a nation like no other and that the God with whom she was in covenant was a God like no other. They were, therefore, always mindful of what was going on in Israel and always drawing conclusions about Israel and her God. Sadly, Israel often gave the impression that the Lord was not real and that she was not unique. When she did so, God would bring judgement upon her to prove those very things. At this time, the nation was again giving her neighbors the wrong ideas. But if she were to return, those very neighbors would consider her to be both 'blessed' and 'a delightful land'."

"Surely, we are driven to ask ourselves a very disturbing question. Can outsiders see God's hand of blessing on us? Does this not explain why our evangelistic efforts have such little impact? If God's hand of blessing were obvious in our lives, unbelievers would be beating a path to our door. But God does not bless disobedience, and disobedience is rampant among Christians. Failure to contribute financially is one act of disobedience that deprives us of God's good hand of blessing with all its evangelistic potential... If we look at our bank accounts, we might very well find reasons not to give. But if we look (as we should) at the cross of Christ, we cannot help but give."[79]

Two verses really guide our thinking in understanding the generosity of God. He's looking for people to give his influence to. Luke 16:10 (NASB) sums it up well, "He who is faithful in a very little thing is faithful also in much; and he who is unrighteous in a very little thing is unrighteous also in much." The other truth is found in Matthew 13:12, "For to the one who has, more will be given, and he will have an abundance, but from the one who has not, even what he has will be taken away." This is true for truth, resources, revelation – all the things God gives us. It's not just restricted to money in this passage but includes truth.

Conclusion

God is a generous God. He wants us to know his blessing. To be truly blessed is to know him.

> The Lord bless you and keep you; the Lord make his face to shine upon you and be gracious to you; the Lord lift up his countenance upon you and give you peace. —Numbers 6:24-26

God loves you. He wants to bless you, but in order to receive his blessing, there must be a deep repentance in your life.

---

[79] Ellsworth, 74-75.

Those who sow in tears shall reap with shouts of joy! —Psalm 126:5

This repentance will restore your fellowship with God, your stewardship for the kingdom, and your testimony before the world.

7 | MALACHI 3:13-18
IF YOU LOVE ME, SERVE MY PURPOSE

They shall be mine, says the Lord of hosts, in the day when I make up my treasured possession, and I will spare them as a man spares his son who serves him.
MALACHI 3:17

God's people were living in prosperity and carnal ease, and God had to awaken them to the need of his love. In the book of Malachi, the people's greatest complaint is that looking at their present circumstances, it looks like God doesn't love them and that they are serving God "in vain" (3:14). Remember this is a book with the theme of God's love. God says, "I have loved you" (1:2). The people say, "How have you loved us?" And God basically says, "You're still here. You are not obliterated like Esau." And the argument of the rest of the book is "I still love you, but you don't love me. But if you want to repent and love me..." and God gives the qualities of people with a heart of love for God. He's said, if you love me, enjoy my worship, lead my people, love your spouse, trust my timing, receive my blessing, and in this passage (3:13-4:3) he says: serve my purpose.

What is your purpose? Your purpose is to be conformed to the image of Christ (Rom 8:30) by experiencing the love of Christ (Rom 5:5). God's purpose for believers, both OT and NT, is to be transformed and redeemed to the original image in which God first created us. God wants to transform us into the image of Christ. R.C. Sproul explains how the transformation is ongoing throughout the life of a Christian:

> The instant that true justifying faith is present in the life of the believer, the person begins to change. That change will be evidenced in a life that moves to obedience. Good works necessarily flow out of true faith. The works do not justify us. It is the righteousness of Christ that justifies us. But if the works do not follow, it is proof positive that we do not have genuine faith and are therefore still unjustified people.[80]

We Often Doubt God's Love

God's love is unearned. We often doubt God's love because of our feelings, our circumstances, our bad behavior, or the settled feeling that we do not measure up. We feel we've sinned too much to be worthy of God's love. Yet, if we look at the underlying motive behind most of our doubts, it's likely self-doubt, self-righteousness, self-pity, and so on. We don't experience God's love because our eyes are on ourselves. What we are going to see in this study is that if we want to experience the love of God, we must fix our eyes on Jesus (Heb 12:1-2). The answer to all the complaints in the book of Malachi is to intensely gaze upon Jesus on the cross, and let the love of God and the assurance of his deep love for you pour into your heart. We cannot experience God's love if we are wanting to be filled with something else. It could be good things or bad things. Some think that if they are filled with enough correct doctrine, they will experience the love of God. D. Martin Lloyd Jones said, "I spend half my time telling Christians to study doctrine and the other half telling them that doctrine is not enough."[81] We need correct doctrine but correct doctrine alone is not enough to experience the love of God. There must be something more. Believing God loves us as he says in the Bible is "good news." What is the good news or the Gospel? It is that God loved us so much he sent Christ to die in our place (Jn 3:16).

---

[80] R.C. Sproul. *Pleasing God* (Wheaton, IL: Tyndale House Publishers, 1994), 153.

[81] T. Sargent. *Gems from Martyn Lloyd-Jones: An Anthology of Quotations from 'the Doctor'* (Milton Keynes, England; Colorado Springs, CO; Hyderabad, AP: Paternoster, 2007), 95-98.

Certainly, the people of Malachi's day had correct doctrine for the most part (though they were leaving it as they married pagan women). They were religious. They followed the Jewish ceremonies. They tried to bring sacrifices to God in the Temple. But they were so far from God. What was missing? They were not experiencing the love of God. By missing the love of God, they were missing authentic worship. They saw their worship as a drudgery. Trying to worship God without experiencing his love is like trying to take a trip down the highway in your vehicle without any fuel. It's impossible. You can't go anywhere without fuel.

Ways We Doubt God's Love

What are some ways we doubt the love of God? Thomas Brooks[82] once identified several ways in which a Christian may doubt God's love. We always doubt God's love when we put our eyes on ourselves. I doubt God's love when...

- I think about my sin more than my Savior (self-loathing).
- I am so distressed at my relapses into sin—even sins I have labored to overcome—and fear they are evidence that I am not a believer (self-focus).
- I feel like I need to do better and try harder to deserve God's love (self-righteousness).
- I mistake my lack of assurance of salvation for a lack of God's love. I feel bad about myself, so God must feel bad about me too (self-pity).
- I think because bad things are happening to me God must not love me (self-condemnation).
- I fear because I have less joy now than I did when I was first saved, so God must not love me (self-scrupulousness).

All of the above are examples have a common theme running through them. Self. Wherever self is there is pride. Humility is not thinking less of yourself, but thinking of yourself less (C.S. Lewis). It's looking at the cross and being so amazed at his love that you forget yourself. I need to turn my eyes upon Jesus and look full in his wonderful face instead of fixing my eyes on myself.

---

[82] Thomas Brooks. *Precious Remedies Against Satan's Devices* (Carlisle, PA: Banner of Truth, 2000), 142-178. First published in 1652.

God's love is not based on myself. It's not based on my behavior, my assurance of salvation, my worthiness, or my righteousness. I look at the cross – my behavior put Christ there. I will never be worthy. The love of God is not based on my goodness, but God's goodness. My sin is paid for in full. That reality should fill me with the love of God.

We often tend to look for things to fill the void in our hearts when we don't experience God's love. Often we think, "If I can get this resolved and that area of sin under control, and if I get this and that together in my life, then I'll be happy." This is an illusion. You and I will never have a completely fulfilled and happy life on earth. There will always be a large measure of unfulfillment in this life. There will be times and seasons both of joy and sorrow, fulfillment and emptiness on earth. When will everything be resolved and my sinful heart healed completely? When Jesus comes again.

You are going to be so heart-sick every day, and you're going to blame it on your marriage, blame it on your circumstances and a thousand other things. You'll say, "If only I had this and that right in my life, then everything would be ok." Not true. You can resolve everything you possibly can on this earth, but you will still have a heart that is homesick for Christ. You can get everything you think you need together, and you will still feel incomplete. Why? Because you as a child of God are homesick for heaven. You are longing for that day when you will no longer have a propensity to sin. You will be totally free. But until then, we are on an imperfect path to perfection. We will only be perfect when Jesus comes. In this passage of Malachi (3:13-15), God says, "If you love me, serve my purpose."

What is Our Purpose?

What then is our purpose in life? When we talk about having purpose in your life, we are not talking about gimmicks (i.e. 40 Days of Purpose). When we talk about purpose, we are referring to what we are created for. As the catechism says, "What is the chief end [i.e. purpose] of man?" Answer: "To glorify God and to love him forever." Our purpose is to glorify God in all we do. "Whether therefore you eat or drink, or whatever you do, do all to the glory of God" (1 Cor 10:31). God's purpose in all things is to conform us to the image of Christ. "And we know that for those who love God all things work together for good, for those who are called according to his purpose....to be conformed to the image of his Son..." (Rom 8:28-29).

OUR PURPOSE IS NOT EARTHLY (3:15-17)

The people in Malachi's day were focused on the here and now where the ungodly rich were outwardly prospering, and God's people were barely surviving. They are doubting God's love because they don't realize that God's purpose is not mainly external prosperity, but internal transformation. God is working on our hearts and our character to conform us to Christ in the midst of a very broken world. Listen to the charge God brings in Malachi 3:

Malachi 3:13-15 | Your words have been hard against me, says the Lord. But you say, 'How have we spoken against you?' You have said, 'It is vain to serve God. What is the profit of our keeping his charge or of walking as in mourning before the Lord of hosts? And now we call the arrogant blessed. Evildoers not only prosper but they put God to the test and they escape'.

How shocking it is to hear God's people say that it is "vain to serve God" because they see no immediate profit or gratification from it. What's the problem with the focus of God's people? Where is their attention? They are fixated on external, earthly circumstances, not on what God wants to do in their hearts. Injustice thrives on the earth. Externally the godly often suffer and the wicked often prosper. People everywhere mock God and prosper. They put God to the test, and yet they seem to escape from his judgment. So the people of Malachi's day conclude, "It's vain to serve God. There is no profit in worshipping him." But they miss the point. Serving God is not about external prosperity but inward transformation. What a sad, selfish existence it is to have as one's life's goal a life with as little pain as possible on earth. Is that our measure of God's blessing? Certainly not.

Progressive Sanctification is Not Earthly

What is the profit in serving God? Today theologians would call it "progressive sanctification." Slowly, and often painfully, we are being conformed into the image of Christ. "If we suffer, we shall also reign with him" (2 Tim 2:12, KJV). Suffering is an important part of the Christian life to help us to grow in Christ. "Beloved, do not be surprised at the fiery trial when it comes upon you to test you, as though something strange were happening to you. But rejoice insofar as you share Christ's sufferings, that you may also rejoice and be glad when his glory is revealed" (1 Pet 4:12-13). Jerry Bridges said, "Our suffering has meaning and purpose in God's eternal plan, and he brings or allows to come into our lives only that which is for his glory and our good."[83] That purpose is to use the chisel of trials and difficulties to restore the image of God in us. The Christian is content to suffer through trials and hardships in this life because we know that God's purpose is to form good character in us. In the end we will reign with Christ and be rewarded, and even that is completely unmerited and undeserved. So when the righteous suffer and the wicked prosper, what are we to do? "Count it all joy, my brothers, when you meet trials of various kinds, for you know that the testing of your faith produces steadfastness. And let steadfastness have its full effect, that you may be perfect and complete, lacking in nothing" (Jas 1:2-4). In this life, we are promised great tribulation. Remember the words of our Lord, "In the world you will have tribulation. But take heart; I have overcome the world" (Jn 16:33).

God's Plan Doesn't Make Sense on Earth

Often the sufferings, tragedies and difficulties of life don't make sense. In a way, all the pressures of life are like a big block of marble that God as the sculptor is working on. All the hitting on the marble doesn't make sense unless you are the artist. An artist in Florence, Italy once asked the great Renaissance sculptor Michelangelo what he saw when he approached a huge block of marble. The famous sculptor stood back and looked at that big square block of white marble, rubbed his chin thoughtfully, and replied, "I see a beautiful form trapped inside, and it is my responsibility to take my mallet and chisel and chip away until the figure is set free." I love that illustration because you can relate to it. Inside of us is a beautiful form, right? Colossians 1:27 says so. It speaks of the hidden figure inside of each believer longing to be "set free." It is "Christ in you, the hope of glory." It's within us, like a seed, like a possibility, like a potential; it's what you hope for: Christ in you glorified through your life, right? The idea is there and our heavenly Father is a little like a sculptor. He wants to release his Son in us. And so, he uses affliction like a hammer and trouble just like a chisel, and he chips and cuts away at us through trials to reveal Jesus' image in you

---

[83] Jerry Bridges. *Trusting God: Even When Life Hurts* (Colorado Springs: Nav-Press, 2008), 21.

and me. God chooses as his model his Son, Jesus Christ because Romans 8:29 says: "For those God foreknew he also predestined to be conformed to the likeness of his Son."

I don't need to tell you that you, and I have lot of hard marble in my life that needs to be chipped away before Christ can be seen in me. We all have that marble. That hammer hurts, doesn't it? Those trials, that chisel bites! After time, the rough form begins to take shape. What does this sculpture look like? God uses suffering to purge sin out of your life and strengthen your commitment to him, and force us to depend on His grace. God uses affliction to bind you together with other believers, produce discernment, and foster sensitivity toward others who hurt. God's got the hammer and chisel in hand to help discipline your minds, teach you to spend your time wisely. That hammer and chisel make you dig deep in God's Word to find comfort. The pain of God's hammer increases your faith and strengthens your character. It creates a beautiful image: Christ in you. All of this happens through trials and suffering. The wicked may prosper, but God is not working in them. God is working in us through much difficulty and tribulation. His purpose is internal, not external. It is heavenly, not earthly.

Earth is the Wrong Place to Fix our Focus

The earthly minded look at the here and now. For them it is vain to serve God because they measure their service by earthly, and immediate results. They see evildoers prosper and attribute the blame to God. Our view as Christians is not earthly but heavenly. Our hope is not in the here and now, but in the moment Christ returns. "If then you have been raised with Christ, seek the things that are above, where Christ is, seated at the right hand of God. Set your minds on things that are above, not on things that are on earth. For you have died, and your life is hidden with Christ in God. When Christ who is your life appears, then you also will appear with him in glory" (Col 3:1-4). Evil doers may prosper here and now for a moment, but they will suffer forever. The godly suffer here and now, but in eternity we will "shall shine like the brightness of the sky above; and those who turn many to righteousness, like the stars forever and ever" (Dan 12:3).

Asaph had the same difficulty with the prosperity of the wicked, and he reached the same conclusion in Psalm 73. "Truly God is good to Israel, to those who are pure in heart. But as for me, my feet had almost stumbled, my steps had nearly slipped. For I was envious of the arrogant when I saw the prosperity of the wicked" (vs. 1-3). The light eventually went on for Asaph. "But when I thought how to understand this, it seemed to me a wearisome task, until I went into the sanctuary of God; then I discerned their end" (vs. 16-17). Once Asaph understood that the vapor of life is so short and eternity is so long, his purpose was clear and his confusion vanished. Paul also understood this same truth: "For I consider that the sufferings of this present time are not worth comparing with the glory that is to be revealed to us" (Rom 8:18).

Faith's Ultimate Reward is Not on Earth

The people of Malachi's day had a wrong focus. Do you hear what they say?

Malachi 3:14 | It is vain to serve God.

They want immediate gratification. They want an earthly satisfaction. Their focus is on earthly prosperity. But not so for the godly. We look beyond earthly things. We are called to "fix our eyes on Jesus" (Heb 12:1). Isaiah says the same thing: "You will keep in perfect peace all who trust in you, all whose thoughts are fixed on you!" (Isa 26:3, NLT).

We need to understand just like Malachi's hearers that faith is often not rewarded on earth. We read of the "hall of faith" in Hebrews 11, and we realize they did not get what God promised until they went to heaven. "These all died in faith, not having received the things promised, but having seen them and greeted them from afar, and having acknowledged that they were strangers and exiles on the earth" (Heb 11:13). Our faith is rewarded in heaven. One day we will hear the Father say, "Well done, good and faithful servant. You have been faithful over a little; I will set you over much. Enter into the joy of your master" (Mt 23:25). When you come right down to our service for God, we find our purpose in Christ. Why would God tell us "Well done, good and faithful servant"? We are not entirely good (having sin that still remains in us), nor are we perfectly faithful. Yet God can rightly say "well done" to every Christian because of our union with Jesus Christ. We are united to him. God rewards us based on what Christ has done in and through us and for us.

Evil's Ultimate Reward is Not on Earth
God's people complain.

Malachi 3:15 | Evildoers not only prosper but they put God to the test, and they escape.

This is wrong on its face. Will anyone escape the justice of God? This question is answered in chapter 4:1, "The day that is coming shall set them ablaze, says the Lord of hosts, so that it will leave them neither root nor branch." No one escapes Judgment Day. We will look at that more in depth in a moment.

OUR PURPOSE IS HEAVENLY (3:16-18)

The people of Malachi's day were focused on external, dry ceremonies when they should have been focused on the intimacy those ceremonies pointed to. God doesn't want robots fulfilling his commands. Our purpose is to know God intimately. We are to "seek first the kingdom of God and his righteousness" and the Lord will take care of the rest of our needs (Mt 6:33). The prophet Malachi gives a beautiful encouragement for those who put the Lord first.

Malachi 3:16a | Then those who feared the Lord spoke with one another. The Lord paid attention and heard them.

God will never forget his people. He loves them and cares for them. A book of remembrance is written in the presence of God to commemorate the people he loves.

A Heavenly People
Who are "those who feared the Lord"? Those who feared the Lord are not necessarily a different group from those who had been complaining, but they are those who have taken the rebuke, and they begin to encourage each other to renewed faith. It is this groping after faith that the Lord heeded and heard. The book of remembrance recorded not righteous deeds, but the names of those who feared the Lord and thought on his name.[84] In other words, the ones who feared the Lord are all true believers from all time.

---

[84] Baldwin, 273.

A Heavenly Book

God is having a book written with the names and perhaps times of fellowship they shared with each other and with God. God pays attention to this. God knows all, but he pays special attention to the sweet love relationship we have with him and with each other.

Malachi 3:16b-17 | A book of remembrance was written before him of those who feared the Lord and esteemed his name. 'They shall be mine, says the Lord of hosts, in the day when I make up my treasured possession, and I will spare them as a man spares his son who serves him.

What is this "book of remembrance"? The kings and nations surrounding Israel in Malachi's day would preserve the happenings of the time with both public and private records. In Malachi 3:16, the Sovereign LORD and King orders a memorandum be etched in this book, likely a stone cylinder common in that day for official records. What were the contents of the memorandum recorded on the cylinder? The contents of the "book of remembrance," it seems, is an official decree to spare those who have an affectionate reverence for the Lord. On the day of God's visitation and judgment (4:1), when Jesus Christ comes in "flaming fire taking vengeance on those who know not God," those who have put their trust in the Lord will be spared (1 Thess 1:8; *cf* Mal 3:17).[85] Instead of being held accountable for their sins, they will be spared as God's "treasured possession."

There are many similarities between the book of remembrance and the book of life. Some scholars believe they are referring to the same thing, or at least the same principle that God's people are known by him. The Bible has much to say about the book of life. "And if anyone's name was not found written in the book of life, he was thrown into the lake of fire" (Rev 20:15). "Nevertheless, do not rejoice in this, that the spirits are subject to you, but rejoice that your names are recorded in heaven" (Lk 10:20). "There will be a time of distress such as never occurred since there was a nation until that time; and at that time your people, everyone who is found written in the book, will be rescued" (Dan 12:1). "Indeed, true companion, I ask you also to help these

[85] David C. Deuel. *Malachi 3:16 – Book of Remembrance or Royal Memorandum?*
(Sun Valley, CA: The Master's Seminary Journal 7/1, Spring 1996), 107-111.

women who have shared my struggle in the cause of the gospel, together with Clement also and the rest of my fellow workers, whose names are in the book of life" (Phil 4:3). "He who overcomes will thus be clothed in white garments; and I will not erase his name from the book of life, and I will confess his name before my Father and before his angels" (Rev 3:5). How amazing it is that God writes us down in his book of remembrance.

The point of God having a "book of remembrance" is to have a list of those he will spare in the Day of Judgment. "I will spare them as a man spares his son who serves him" (3:17). Anyone with children knows that our sons and daughters make plenty of mistakes. There are many sinful actions. Depending on the day, all of God's people fall short of God's perfect standard, except for one Son. We are spared not because we have been faithful sons and daughters, but because Christ has been the faithful Son, and we are united to him. Certainly, those who are united with Christ serve God faithfully, but not perfectly.

A Heavenly Delight

God says of believers: "They shall be mine ... I will spare them" (3:17). We as blood bought believers are heaven's delight. As we meditate on the passage, it becomes clear that the ones written in God's book have certain qualities. They have certain marks. Malachi is making a distinction between the righteous and the wicked (3:18). This is common throughout the Bible, especially in the writings of Paul, Peter and John. Paul is constantly giving qualities that distinguish the saved and the lost (i.e. Gal 5, 1 Cor 6) as is Peter (2 Pet 1:3-11). St. John dedicates an entire letter to distinguishing those who are children of the light and those who are children of the devil (cf. 1 Jn). It is no surprise to then to see them imitating Malachi and other prophets who give us the qualities of those who are written in God's book.

1. We fear the Lord. As God's people, we have an "affectionate reverence" toward him. As sinful people, we have every reason to fear God's judgment, but that is not at all what this fear is. We are people who have been forgiven, and we now have what Martin Luther called a *filial* (from the Latin meaning family) fear. A filial fear refers to "the fear that a child has for his father. In this regard, Luther said it's like a child who has tremendous respect and love for his father or mother and who dearly wants to please them. He has a fear or an anxiety of offend-

ing the one he loves, not because he's afraid of torture or even of punishment, but rather because he's afraid of displeasing the one who is, in that child's world, the source of security and love."[86] We fear displeasing the Lord who loves us. That's the kind of fear we have.

2. We esteem and think upon the name of the Lord. As Christians we love to meditate on his name. "The 'name' of God is his self-revelation; his word. So the Lord assured believers, those who truly reverenced God and possessed God-consciousness, that they would not be forgotten."[87] God has revealed himself as our protection, salvation, health, purpose and destiny. Jump into his name like a child would jump into their Daddy's arms. He is our "Abba, Father."

3. We meet together and speak to one another. God's pattern for producing people with powerful faith and genuine love is not to have the pastor-teachers do all the work of the ministry. They are to equip the saints to do the ministry (Eph 4:11-12). We are called to meet together and speak together about the Lord. "Let us hold fast the confession of our hope without wavering, for he who promised is faithful. And let us consider how to stir up one another to love and good works, not neglecting to meet together, as is the habit of some, but encouraging one another, and all the more as you see the Day drawing near" (Heb 10:23-25). Christ himself had said earlier to the apostle John and the other eleven disciples, "By this all people will know that you are my disciples, if you have love for one another" (Jn 13:35). There are over thirty-five commands in the New Testament for Christians to live life together and serve "one another." 1 John 5:1, "Everyone who loves the Father loves whoever has been born of him." We love one another and speak to one another for mutual edification.

4. We are God's treasured possession, his precious "jewels" (KJV). This term "designates a rare possession of God, select from among all others (Exo 19:5; Deut 7:6; 14:2; 26:18; Psa 135:4), or some special object of a king (1 Chron 29:3; Eccl. 2:8)."[88] We belong to the Lord. We are knit into his heart. "The LORD your God is in your midst, a mighty one who will save; he will rejoice over you with gladness; he will quiet

---

[86] R.C. Sproul. *What Does it Mean to Fear God?* (Sanford, FL: Ligonier Ministries, Oct 22, 2016), www.ligonier.org/blog/what-does-it-mean-fear-god, Accessed 3 March 2017.

[87] Smith, *Minor Prophets*, Mal 3:16.

[88] Baker, 296.

you by his love; he will exult over you with loud singing" (Zeph 3:17). "See, I have written your name on the palms of my hands" (Isa 49:16, NLT). "They are my jewels" (3:17, KJV), says the Lord. What a beautiful picture of the faithful believer. Jewels are precious, and we are precious in his sight. He purchased us with his blood. He is polishing us with trials and testings; and one day in glory we shall shine in beauty and splendor.[89]

A Heavenly Distinction

Throughout the Bible we hear about the "righteous" and the "wicked."

Malachi 3:18 | Then once more you shall see the distinction between the righteous and the wicked, between one who serves God and one who does not serve him.

The Lord knows those who are his. The distinction between the righteous and the wicked is one of holiness. The deepest desire of the Christian is to "abide in Christ" and to "keep his word." Fellowship with God expresses itself in the choices and decisions of the believer. In the Old Testament, this concept is called, "the fear of the Lord." There is a holy reverence and love that produces obedience. Solomon said, "The end of the matter; all has been heard. Fear God and keep his command-ments, for this is the whole duty of man" (Eccl 12:13). "The fear of the LORD is the beginning of wisdom, and the knowledge of the Holy One is insight" (Pro 9:10). Moses said, "Show me your glory" (Exo 33:18). The righteous' "delight is in the law of the Lord, and on his law he meditates day and night. He is like a tree planted by streams of water that yields its fruit in its season, and its leaf does not wither. In all that he does, he prospers. The wicked are not so, but are like chaff that the wind drives away. Therefore, the wicked will not stand in the judgment, nor sinners in the congregation of the righteous; for the Lord knows the way of the righteous, but the way of the wicked will perish" (Psa 1:2-6).

The Distinction in the Book of Proverbs

The five books of Moses (Pentateuch) and much of the wisdom lit-erature (Psalms, Proverbs, Ecclesiastes) have a distinction between the

---

[89] Warren Wiersbe. *Wiersbe's Expository Outlines on the Old Testament* (Wheaton, IL: Victor Books, 1993), Mal 3:1-15.

righteous and the wicked. We might call it the "principle of the path." In the book of Proverbs the first nine chapters are lectures to the son. In those chapters he is given two paths over and over again: the path of the wicked and the pathway of the righteous. Sometimes it is called the path of Lady Wisdom and the path of Lady Folly. The principle of the book of Proverbs is: *You can choose your path, but you cannot choose your destination.* In other words, if I want to go to Chicago, I need to take I-55 North. If I want to reach Louisiana, I need to take I-55 South. I can say I want to go to Chicago while on I-55 South all day long, but at the end of the day, if I go South, I'm headed to Louisiana. The only way I can change my course is by changing directions. I do that by making new choices. The Bible calls that repentance. The book of Proverbs constantly warn us that our choices determine our path. Here are some examples: The path of the righteous: "Trust in the Lord with all your heart, and do not lean on your own understanding. In all your ways acknowledge him, and he will make straight your paths" (Pro 3:5-6). The path of the wicked: "My son, be attentive to my wisdom; incline your ear to my understanding, that you may keep discretion, and your lips may guard knowledge. For the lips of a forbidden woman drip honey, and her speech is smoother than oil, but in the end she is bitter as wormwood, sharp as a two-edged sword. Her feet go down to death; her steps follow the path to Sheol; she does not ponder the path of life; her ways wander, and she does not know it" (Pro 5:1-6).

One pathway brings us to God, and the other pathway brings us to death and the grave. A person can say, "I want a godly spouse, a godly home, a godly life." But if they are choosing fornication, selfish living, and making bad choices, their path is wicked, and they are headed to death and hell. It's not my words that determine my path but my choices. The righteous person on the other hand generally chooses the good path. It's not that the righteous person is perfect. This is clear from the wisdom literature of the Bible. "Though he fall, he shall not be utterly cast down: for the LORD upholdeth him with his hand" (Psa 37:24, KJV). "The righteous falls seven times and rises again" (Pro 24:16).In other words, the righteous are on a pathway of pleasing God that leads to progressive sanctification. The wicked are on a pathway of pleasing self that leads to death and the grave. Throughout the Bible, we hear of the "wicked" and the "righteous." "There is none righteous, no not one" (Rom 3:11). The righteous are those on the pathway seeking the Lord. The wicked are those who go another pathway to a different destination – one of destruction.

The Distinction in the Book of Malachi

The point of what Malachi is saying is simple: there is "a distinction between the righteous and the wicked, between the one who serves God and the one who doesn't." There is a tenderness of heart, a trust, in the one who serves God. He knows the goodness of God and speaks of him to others who fear the Lord. There is an affectionate reverence for the Lord. In other words, serving God is not mere action, but proceeds from the motives of the heart. Many of the people of Malachi's day did not have a love for God and did not experience God's love, like those who feared the Lord. Trust in the Lord and tenderness of heart make all the difference. The wicked may participate in external ceremonies, but their heart is far from God. The righteous certainly have the outward forms and formality of religion, but they also have an intimate relationship with the Lord, and that makes all the difference. It is that relationship which is proof they are written in God's book and will be spared on the day of his visitation in judgment. God visited the earth once by sending his Son Jesus Christ in order to condemn sin. He will come again to spare believers and bring condemnation against those without Christ.

Conclusion

We must never forget that God's purpose is not mainly external, but internal, conforming us to the image of Christ through experiencing his love. You will want to seek after earthly goals, which are perfectly fine. It is good to have ambitions for education, marriage, career, etc., but remember God's ultimate purpose is none of these things. He wants to use the pressure in all those things to conform you to Jesus. Never, never forget that. It is good to serve God in the programs and methods of the church, but never forget that God's purpose is that you know him intimately. We can be immersed in God's work without having a walk with God. Don't miss your purpose. The consequences of who or what you live for are eternal.

8 | MALACHI 4:4-6

IF YOU LOVE ME, WAIT FOR MY SON

*But for you who fear my name, the sun of righteousness
shall rise with healing in its wings. You shall go out leaping
like calves from the stall.*
MALACHI 4:2

Waiting is not easy. We long for things to be made right. We yearn for our tears to be wiped away. Something is wrong in the universe. Who will fix it? A day is coming when the Lord will restore all things as new. The Father in heaven is sending Messiah soon – so Malachi tells the people of his day. Messiah is coming. Be faithful to wait for him, because without the sacrifice of Jesus God would meticulously meet out judgment. "I will come and strike the land with a decree of utter destruction." That's the last sentence in the Old Testament. It doesn't sound hopeful, but it is. We could paraphrase the last sentence in the old covenant from a New Testament perspective like this: "Unless Jesus comes, there will be utter doom for you." Utter. Doom. Here's the point: we need Jesus.

THE WICKED AWAIT GOD'S WRATH (4:1)

Malachi 4:1 | 'For behold, the day is coming, burning like an oven, when all the arrogant and all evildoers will be stubble. The day that is coming shall set them ablaze, says the Lord of hosts, so that it will leave them neither root nor branch.

What day is the prophet recalling? There can be no doubt that Malachi was referring to the day which he mentioned in the last verse of chapter 3, that is, the Day of Judgment. God is like a refiner's fire to the believer, bringing the heart and crucible of trials to the believer's life in order to purify his children. But to the unbeliever, God is like the destructive fire of an oven that burns so hot, there will be "neither root nor branch." The prophet compares it to the burning of a furnace and likens the wicked to stubble and shrubs that will be unable to stand the fire of that terrible day.[90] In other words, God's punishment cannot be withstood or escaped from. There are no exits in hell.

The Swiftness of God's Wrath

We don't like to think about it, but the Day of Judgment is coming. All unbelievers will suddenly be like chaff in a burning furnace. "When the stubble hits the oven, it is burned, and when the wicked hit judgment, they are consumed."[91] As the writer of Hebrews warned: "Our God is a consuming fire" (Heb 12:29, KJV). Jonathan Edwards described this scene on Judgment Day in frightening, yet accurate terms. He said God is not "unmindful" of the wickedness of sinners. He is not like them at all, but is pained by wickedness and must punish it. God is not forgetful as the lost imagine him to be. Listen to Edwards describe God's wrath.

> The wrath of God burns against them, their damnation don't slumber, the pit is prepared, the fire is made ready, the furnace is now hot, ready to receive them, the flames do now rage and glow. The glittering sword is whet [sharpened], and held over them, and the pit hath opened her mouth under them."[92]

These words are not at all different from what Malachi was warning God's people about. "For behold, the day is coming, burning like an

---

[90] W. A. VanGemeren. *Malachi*. In *Evangelical Commentary on the Bible*, Vol. 3 (Grand Rapids, MI: Baker Book House, 1995), 711.

[91] Ellsworth., 84-85.

[92] Jonathan Edwards. *Sinners in the Hands of an Angry God* (Edinburgh: Lumisden and Robertson, 1745), 10. *Archived copy from the British Museum.* (Sermon preached July 8, 1741 in Enfield, MA)

oven" (4:1a). God has not forgotten the wicked as the people of Malachi's day imagined. Remember they charged God with forgetting the wicked? They said, "Evildoers not only prosper but they put God to the test and they escape'" (3:17). God is answering this false accusation. Indeed, there is a day coming in which God will judge the wicked. St. John gives us a front seat vision of that last day when all are judged: "Then I saw a great white throne and him who was seated on it. From his presence earth and sky fled away, and no place was found for them. And I saw the dead, great and small, standing before the throne, and books were opened. Then another book was opened, which is the book of life. And the dead were judged by what was written in the books, according to what they had done. And the sea gave up the dead who were in it, Death and Hades gave up the dead who were in them, and they were judged, each one of them, according to what they had done. Then Death and Hades were thrown into the lake of fire. This is the second death, the lake of fire. And if anyone's name was not found written in the book of life, he was thrown into the lake of fire" (Rev 20:11-15). God will "set them ablaze" (4:1). Jesus will come "in flaming fire taking vengeance on those who know not God and obey not the Gospel of our Lord Jesus Christ" (1 Thess 1:8).

The Reality of God's Wrath

Jesus speaks to the multitude gathered about the most tragic calamity that any human being can experience. It is not physical death. It is rather being "cast into hell." "I tell you, my friends, do not fear those who kill the body, and after that have nothing more that they can do. But I will warn you whom to fear: fear him who, after he has killed, has authority to cast into hell. Yes, I tell you, fear him!" (Lk 12:4-5). The word translated "hell" is the Greek word "Gehenna." The word was the name of the city refuse dump where the fires unceasingly burned. It is a frightening representation of that which awaits those without God.[93] There is much about hell that we do not know. But the story of the rich man and the beggar named Lazarus in Luke 16 reveals much. "There was a rich man who was clothed in purple and fine linen and who feasted sumptuously every day. And at his gate was laid a poor man named Lazarus, covered with sores, who desired to be fed with what fell from the rich man's table. Moreover, even the dogs came and licked

---

[93] Ellsworth, 85.

his sores. The poor man died and was carried by the angels to Abraham's side. The rich man also died and was buried, and in Hades, being in torment, he lifted up his eyes and saw Abraham far off and Lazarus at his side. And he called out, 'Father Abraham, have mercy on me, and send Lazarus to dip the end of his finger in water and cool my tongue, for I am in anguish in this flame.' But Abraham said, 'Child, remember that you in your lifetime received your good things, and Lazarus in like manner bad things; but now he is comforted here, and you are in anguish. And besides all this, between us and you a great chasm has been fixed, in order that those who would pass from here to you may not be able, and none may cross from there to us.' And he said, 'Then I beg you, father, to send him to my father's house— for I have five brothers—so that he may warn them, lest they also come into this place of torment.' But Abraham said, 'They have Moses and the Prophets; let them hear them.' And he said, 'No, father Abraham, but if someone goes to them from the dead, they will repent.' He said to him, 'If they do not hear Moses and the Prophets, neither will they be convinced if someone should rise from the dead'" (Lk 16:19-31). From this passage we understand: (1) Hell is a real place. (2) It is a place of separation from God and all that is good (Lk 16:23). (3) It is a place of just punishment (Lk 16:24). (4) It is a place where there is memory (Lk 16:25). (5) It is a place of hopelessness (Lk 16:26). Something else we know is that believers in Christ do not have to go to hell. Those who trust in Jesus as Savior and Lord will be saved. The coming day of judgment will be a day of great rejoicing for the redeemed (Rom 8:1).

THE RIGHTEOUS AWAIT JESUS' HEALING (4:2-3)

Malachi 4:2a | But for you who fear my name, the sun of righteousness shall rise with healing in its wings.

The church fathers from Justin onward have almost universally understood the "sun of righteousness" to be Christ.[94] Martin Luther in particular said, "Under the Law there is weakness and condemnation; under the wings of Christ, under the Gospel, there is strength and salvation."[95] Whereas when we were lost, the guilt and shame of our trans-

---

[94] Boice. 611.

[95] Luther, *Luther's Works,* Vol. 18, *Lectures on the Minor Prophets,* 418.

gressions against God's law flew over us like a pack of vultures indicating death, so God's grace and love pursue his children like a winged sun, representing the desire of God's heart to do good to unworthy people.

Healed By a Winged Sun

The Old Testament closes with the promise of the rising of the winged "sun of righteousness." The New Testament closes with the promise of the rising of the "morning star" (Rev 22:16).[96] What is this winged sun? The symbol of the winged sun was so powerful in the hearts of ancient believers that it was adopted by some of the Hebrew kings, most noteworthy of which is Hezekiah. In 2015, the royal seal of King Hezekiah's signet right was discovered on the grounds of the royal palace in Jerusalem.[97] It reads, "Hezekiah, Son of Ahaz, King of Judah." There is an "Ankh" which is a cross with a circle at the top. It is the most ancient symbol in human writing which symbolizes "eternal life." But there is also the symbol of the winged sun – a symbol that God's grace and protection will follow you wherever you go. This was a very common symbol that the prophet Malachi refers to in Malachi 4. We see it in the sketch of Hezekiah's signet ring below.

The famous signet ring of Hezekiah, son of Ahaz, king of Judah

The symbol of the winged sun goes back to 2000 BC in Egypt where it represented the sun god and the Pharaoh.

---

[96] K. Brooks *Summarized Bible: Complete Summary of the Old Testament* (Bellingham, WA: Logos Bible Software, 2009), 215.

[97] Meir Lubetski. *King Hezekiah's Seal Revisited* (Washington, DC: Biblical Archeology Review, July/August 2001 – 24/7), 44.

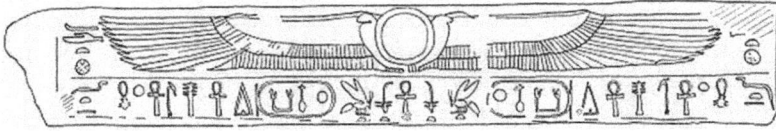

The Egyptian winged sun disk (Parayre 1990: plate 1, no. 1)

Why would Hezekiah use an ancient pagan symbol from Egypt for his reign? And why would Malachi use this symbol to point to the coming Messiah? In view of the Old Testament Scriptures' description of Yahweh in several passages as an infinite God with cosmic features, wings, and one whose name derives from a verb meaning 'to be,' we can begin to comprehend the reasons the Judean royalty might have appropriated such a symbol. The winged sun effectively served the purpose of promoting the worship of Yahweh alone, principally in his role as the God most high, over against the Assyrian local deities to the North and other Canaanite deities that had infected Israel and Judah, such as Asherah and Baal.[98] The prophet Malachi applies this ancient symbol to the grace of God that follows the child of God.

Malachi 4:2a | But for you who fear my name, the sun of righteousness shall rise with healing in its wings.

In other words, "the sun of God's grace will follow you wherever you go!" The winged sun originating from Egypt was adopted, especially by Hezekiah, as a picture of the eternal, infinite God who gives eternal life. Malachi, reading 2 Chronicles written a hundred years before Malachi by Ezra, would have known about Hezekiah's symbol and uses it as a powerful way to encourage those who truly fear the Lord. What a hopeful message Malachi gave: there is coming a day when God will spare the righteous. His winged sun of righteousness will follow you wherever you go. This blessing reminds us of the Levitical blessing: "The Lord bless you and keep you; the Lord make his face to shine upon you and be gracious to you; the Lord lift up his countenance upon you and give you peace" (Num 6:24-26).

---

[98] Daniel Sarlo, "Winged Scarab Imagery in Judah: Yahweh as Khepri," University of Toronto, 2014. Accessed 15 March 2017, academia.edu/5562359/Winged_Scarab_
Imagery_in_Judah_Yahweh_as_Khepri

Healed Like a Leaping Calf

Malachi 4:2b | You shall go out leaping like calves from the stall.

For the Christian who understands he or she is loved by God, there is such "joy unspeakable and full of glory" (1 Pet 1:8) that inside we feel like a calf that has been freed – jumping and leaping for pure joy. We were in the stall of sin, and one day we will be like calves released into the sunshine from their soiled stalls, kicking up their heels in sheer enthusiasm. Love is powerful. Love is healing. It brings joy back to your heart.

Healed Forever

No longer will the righteous be persecuted. No longer will they suffer needlessly. No longer will sin, the flesh, the devil, and the world system be opposing the sanctification of God's people. It will all be over. The Lamb will triumph and God's people will walk over the ashes of the wicked.

Malachi 4:3 | And you shall tread down the wicked, for they will be ashes under the soles of your feet, on the day when I act, says the Lord of hosts.

Hallelujah! It seems strange to take delight in the destruction of the wicked, and so it is. The emphasis then is not rejoicing at all in the death of the wicked, for God "is not willing that any should perish." But there is coming a day when God must act. We all must be judged. And in that day, the focus is not on death and destruction but on the conquering Lamb.

THE LAW TELLS US TO WAIT IN FAITH (4:4)

Emphasis on the law of Moses (4:4) and on the figure of Elijah (4:5-6) summed up all that God's servants had stood for throughout the centuries since Israel was redeemed from Egypt. When the law and the prophets were put together in one collection of sacred texts, these twin references looked forward to the consummation of the purpose for which both were given.[99] It is only appropriate that the prophet Malachi appeals to the law of Moses and to Elijah, the most prominent prophet of the Old Testament as he closes out the canon.

---

[99] Baldwin, 229.

We know the day Christ's judgement is coming, but what shall we do while we wait? Malachi tells us:

Malachi 4:4 | Remember the law of my servant Moses, the statutes and rules that I commanded him at Horeb for all Israel.

The Biblical commentator, Rabbi Avraham Ibn Ezra (1089-1164), says that it was because there would be no prophets after him that Malachi told the Jews to remember Moses' law.[100] What does Moses' law point to? Man's unrighteousness. It sounds peculiar that Malachi says to remember Sinai. Yet it is Sinai reminds of our need for a Savior. We are so guilty, it is worth waiting for God's "Sun of Righteousness." Horeb is another name for Sinai in the book of Deuteronomy. How frightful God's law was at Sinai. The lightening lit up the sky when God gave Moses the Ten Commandments. The thunder rolled and fire burned furiously on her peak. No one was permitted to come near the base of the mountain upon penalty of death. The Ten Commandments lay out our obligations to God and man. We can't be saved by keeping the commandments. "For by works of the law no human being will be justified in his sight, since through the law comes knowledge of sin" (Rom 3:20).

What is the purpose of God telling us to "remember the law" of Moses? Why would God draw such attention to his terrifying law at Mount Sinai in a prophecy about his love? The law cannot save us, but is like a mirror that shows us our need of Christ. The law, Paul says, is the "schoolmaster" that brings us to Christ (Gal 3:24). This is an especially important tension in the Bible. God is holy. Man is wretched and sinful. We look to God and his law and see ourselves as condemned, overcome with guilt and shame. I deserve hell. My conscience and God's law condemn me. It is this humiliation in the soul that brings us to see our deep need for Christ. Remember the law of Moses! No son of Adam can fulfill it (Rom 3:20). But there is One who has. The Son of God.

Remember Christ's Imputation

The law of Moses, of course, condemns us. The soul that sins shall die. Either I have to die for my sins in hell or a perfect sacrifice has to take my place. When we "remember the law" of Moses, it points us to

---

[100] Abraham Ibn Ezra. *Commentary of Ibn Ezra on Malachi* (London: Society of Hebrew Literature, 1873), Mal 1:1.

what New Testament scholars call "imputation." What is imputation? It is simply this: Jesus lived the life we should have lived, and died the death we should have died. Puritan John Owen explained, "The Lord Christ fulfilled the whole law for us; He did not only undergo the penalty of it due unto our sins, but also yielded that perfect obedience which it did require."[101]

We realize that no human being can keep the law of God righteously. There is only one who is righteous, Jesus. Theologians talk about his obedience for us being active and passive. Jesus perfectly obeyed the law in thought, word and deed in his life (active obedience), and he perfectly satisfied God's wrath in his death (passive obedience). Remember the law! Christ fulfilled it. "For Moses writes about the righteousness that is based on the law, that the person who does the commandments shall live by them" (Rom 10:5). Has anyone done that? Only Jesus Christ! "For we do not have a high priest who is unable to sympathize with our weaknesses, but one who in every respect has been tempted as we are, yet without sin" (Heb 4:15). J. Greshem Machen said, "Every event of Jesus' life was a part of that glorious keeping of the law of God by which he earned for his people the reward of eternal life."[102] So we have good reason to "remember the law." Christ fulfilled it on our behalf.

Remember the Spirit's Law on Your Heart

Of course Christians have a new law in their hearts when they are born again. At the close of the Old Testament we await a new law that comes at Pentecost. The Spirit of God is poured out at Pentecost and now indwells all born again people. These people constitute the "Body of Christ" and the new "Temple." "For through him we both have access in one Spirit to the Father. So then you are no longer strangers and aliens, but you are fellow citizens with the saints and members of the household of God, built on the foundation of the apostles and prophets, Christ Jesus himself being the cornerstone, in whom the whole structure, being joined together, grows into a holy temple in the Lord. In him you also are being built together into a dwelling place for God by the Spirit" (Eph 2:18-22).

---

[101] John Owen. *The Doctrine of Justification by Faith* (London: R. Boulter, 1677), 365.

[102] J. Gresham Machen, "The Active Obedience of Christ," in *God Transcendent* (Edinburgh: Banner of Truth, 1982), 191.

This is consistent with the teaching of Paul in Romans 8:1-4, "There is therefore now no condemnation for those who are in Christ Jesus. For the law of the Spirit of life has set you free in Christ Jesus from the law of sin and death. For God has done what the law, weakened by the flesh, could not do. By sending his own Son in the likeness of sinful flesh and for sin, he condemned sin in the flesh, in order that the righteous requirement of the law might be fulfilled in us, who walk not according to the flesh but according to the Spirit" (cf. Eze 36:25-27). Not only should we wait in faith by remembering the law. We should wait in faith looking for what Elijah and all the prophets were pointing to.

ELIJAH TELLS US TO WAIT IN FAITH (4:5-6a)

Malachi 4:5-6a | Behold, I will send you Elijah the prophet before the great and awesome day of the Lord comes. And he will turn the hearts of fathers to their children and the hearts of children to their fathers...

We know that this prophecy of "Elijah" is pointing to the ministry of John the Baptist (Mt 11:11–14; 17:10–13), and we know that John the Baptist came to pave the way for Jesus (John 1:19–34).[103] It was John who (referring to Malachi 4) cried out: "Behold, the Lamb of God, who takes away the sin of the world! This is he of whom I said, 'After me comes a man who ranks before me, because he was before me'" (Jn 1:29-30).

Jesus interpreted these verses so clearly in Matthew 11:11-15, "Truly, I say to you, among those born of women there has arisen no one greater than John the Baptist. Yet the one who is least in the kingdom of heaven is greater than he. From the days of John the Baptist until now the kingdom of heaven has suffered violence, and the violent take it by force. For all the Prophets and the Law prophesied until John, and if you are willing to accept it, he is Elijah who is to come. He who has ears to hear, let him hear."

Jesus told the Pharisees, "You search the Scriptures because you think that in them you have eternal life; and it is they that bear witness about me" (Jn 5:39). After Jesus' resurrection, Jesus walked the road to Emmaus and one of them named Cleopas explained the unusual

---

[103] Ellsworth, 88.

events of that day. He said, 'Some of those who were with us went to the tomb and found it just as the women had said, but him they did not see.' And he said to them, 'O foolish ones, and slow of heart to believe all that the prophets have spoken! Was it not necessary that the Christ should suffer these things and enter into his glory?' And beginning with Moses and all the Prophets, he interpreted to them in all the Scriptures the things concerning himself" (Lk 24:24-27). All the prophets point to Jesus. So look to where the prophets are pointing.

By the way, the ministry of John the Baptist would prove to have a profound effect on the family life of the people of Israel. It would turn the hearts of fathers towards their children and the hearts of the children towards their fathers. How we need such a turning! And that turning can come only as parents and children find a common bond in the Christ of whom John spoke.

WHAT IF WE DON'T WAIT IN FAITH? (4:6b)

We must look to Jesus through the Law and the Prophets, God says:

Malachi 4:6b | ...lest I come and strike the land with a decree of utter destruction" (4:6b).

John the Baptist comes with a ministry of repentance that will introduce the one who will hold back the curse. If this doesn't happen, then God would have to "come and strike the land with a decree of utter destruction." Without Jesus' coming, we have only judgment to look forward to. But in Christ there is "no condemnation" (Rom 8:1). Without the coming Messiah, there is no hope for mankind.

Epilogue

That's the end of the Old Testament story. But you say, "That can't be the end. That's not a satisfying story." I agree. "That's just the bad news." I agree. It's like Cinderella being left with the evil stepmother in the end. Yes. It's like Snow White being left in the glass coffin. Why don't you tickle our ears with the good news?" Because I can't in the Old Testament. The Old Testament ending leaves us feeling the emptiness of mankind without God. Let's feel the impact of millennia of human history of mankind not being able to reach God on their own. Let's see the devastation of mankind and mankind's kingdoms upon the earth, its oppression, its corruption, and its destructions. Nothing can last. And let the Old Testament story prepare the way for the hopeless-ness of man left to himself. That's what the Old Testament does until something bursts onto the scene. Not something but Someone.

Malachi closes his book and the Old Testament canon and begins a period where prophecy ceases until the voice of John the Baptist is heard. There are unmet expectations, unfulfilled prophecies, and un-satisfied promises. Once Malachi puts down his pen there begins a pe-riod of over four hundred years of silence. No more words will be breathed out by God until the final Word, Jesus comes into the world (Heb 1:1-3). In a tender and genuine sense, God closes out the book of Malachi and the Old Testament and says, "I'm sending Jesus soon. Wait for me! You can be sure he is coming, because *I still love you.*"

Unbeliever, if you are reading this, there is no excuse for you not to turn to Jesus Christ today. What has two thousand plus years of hu-man history showed you? That you're going to do something different? Really? You can't get to God on your own. Jesus Christ is the way to heaven. He loves you.

Believer, there is no excuse for you not to stand boldly now in Christ because he took our punishment for sin and you stand just be-fore a holy God in Christ's righteousness. Be encouraged. That is the good news. When the Old Testament ends on the bad news, Jesus Christ comes in ushering in the good news.

You may obtain this and many other fine resources made available by Proclaim Publishers by contacting us:

Web:
proclaimpublishers.com

Email:
contact@proclaimpublishers.com

Postal Mail:
Proclaim Publishers
PO Box 2082
Wenatchee, WA 98807

S O L I D E O G L O R I A

ISBN 978-1-387-17666-3
9 781387 176663
90000

www.ingramcontent.com/pod-product-compliance
Lightning Source LLC
Chambersburg PA
CBHW021930040426
42448CB00008B/993